T0016038

TANTRA

TANTRA
LIFE-ENHANCING RITUALS OF POWER

HAMRAZ AHSAN

SIRIUS

SIRIUS

This edition published in 2022 by Sirius Publishing, a division of
Arcturus Publishing Limited,
26/27 Bickels Yard, 151–153 Bermondsey Street,
London SE1 3HA

ISBN: 978-1-3988-2098-2
AD008726UK

Printed in China

Contents

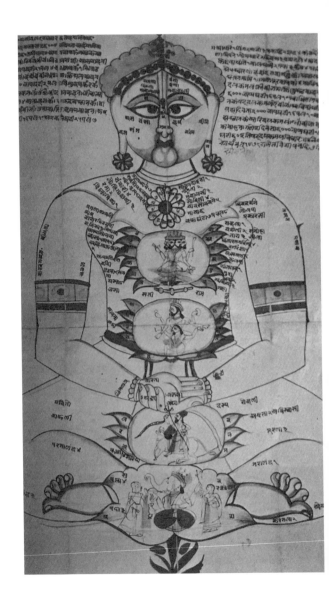

Introduction

'The tantric sages tell us that our
in-breath and out-breath actually
mirror the divine creative gesture.
With the inhalation, we draw into
our own centre, our own being.
With the exhalation, we expand
outward into the world.'

AWAKENING SHAKTI: THE TRANSFORMATIVE
POWER OF THE GODDESSES OF YOGA
SALLY KEMPTON

Tantra is perhaps one of the most misunderstood concepts arising from the scriptures and theologies of the Indian subcontinent. In the west, popular culture has made the word synonymous with esoteric sex acts, which cheapens and belittles a profound body of philosophical knowledge that has more to do with enlightenment than it does with coupling. There is sexuality within tantra – of course, there is! – but it is to a higher purpose than mere enjoyment of bodily pleasure.

What is true about the general understanding of tantra is that it is indeed *esoteric* in nature, a secret ritualistic practice that is embedded in specific Hindu, Buddhist and Jain temples and requires teaching and rituals passed down from guru to disciple over many years. It is this very hidden aspect of tantra that has historically attracted western occultists and informed a lot of their work. Perhaps another attraction was how much orientalists of the British Empire were repulsed by the taboo-breaking nature of some tantric practices and so dismissed all of it as, in the words of the 19th century ethnologist Brian Houghton Hodgson, 'lust, mummery and black magic'. A Bengali writer contemporary to Hodgson, K. Chakravarthi, explained it better: 'Unfortunately [the tantrics'] intentions have been so grossly misrepresented in our days that the very name of tantra shocks our nerves; yet two-thirds of our religious rites are tantric, and almost half our medicine is tantric.' This latter quote is far closer to what tantra is in reality than the one before it. The truth is that when tantric practices are taken out of the wider context of tantric teachings, you get the action without the understanding or motivation behind it. This can lead to much confusion and poor comprehension.

What is tantra?

Imma Ramos, curator at the British Museum, explains that the Sanskrit word 'tantra' comes from the verbal root *tan* meaning to weave or compose. The word refers to a type of scripture that speaks about the nature of existence, outlines rituals that can be performed for a variety of different outcomes, and is often presented as a record of an exchange between a god and goddess.

The god is a representation of Shiva (pictured opposite) and the goddess is a representation of Shakti. What is interesting is that, despite the dual play of masculine and feminine energy, the tantras do not insist upon a gendered approach. This is because ultimately Shiva and Shakti are both Brahman (Ultimate Divinity). Differentiation and duality only come into play so that the Divine may dance with Themself. This is why a purely sexual understanding of tantra is so frustrating and, if one is being clear about this, unnecessarily exclusionary. One doesn't even have to be a sexual being to enjoy the benefits of tantric practices. Our path to spiritual enlightenment is wider than the limits of gender and sex.

While there are tantric scriptures dating back to the sixth century CE, most practitioners believe a practical approach is the one to take. Books can only take you so far on this journey. You may be wondering then why this book exists at all? Here you will find an overview of tantric ideas as well as some practices that begin the journey toward raising your consciousness in the way described within those scriptures. A 'journey' is a good analogy for the practice of tantra in the modern world because you set off to try and reach a destination – that

of pure, ecstatic union with the Divine – but you find
that it isn't a matter of following a straightforward map
and that, in fact, there are many twists and turns along
the way. Sometimes you will feel lost, even as you turn
the corner and see your proximity to the end.

So what is that final destination? Even here, there
is dispute. There are those who call it ultimate union
and those who call it realization. These differences arise
from fundamental philosophical ideas about the nature
of the universe. Is the universe composed of many
individuated beings and things that then meet with the
whole and become One or is everything already One
and all individuation is an illusion (*maya*)? It may be
that both ideas, despite being contradictory, are true.

The way that tantra resolves the issue is by having
the goddess Shakti pose questions on this and having
Shiva, her consort god, answer them. On occasion, he
will ask the question and she give the answer. This way
Divinity witnesses the truth unfold in the cosmos.

How does a mortal human being, who not usually
touched by divine wisdom, come to see the truth?
Strangely enough, in the same way as the gods do.
Through practising the 'yoga of knowledge' – the parts
of yogic teaching concerned with meditation and

awakening kundalini (see page 62) – we too can come
to experience the Oneness of all. This realization is
called *sadhana* and this is also the term for the series of
exercises you undertake to come to it. These comprise
mudras (see chapter four, pages 106-25), mantras and
contemplating yantras (sacred geometric designs that
represent specific gods and goddesses).

The traditional disciple takes years of daily practice
to achieve *sadhana*, but this isn't possible in the modern
world unless you go and train with a tantric temple.
However, the modern person can still enjoy many of
the benefits of these practices and it is said that when
the body and mind are trained sufficiently, the spirit
naturally achieves the heights it is capable of.

Is there any benefit to realizing the true nature of
the world — the *maya* or illusion of all things we take
to be real? The aim is not to become so extraordinarily
awakened that you are no longer capable of living life,
more that you understand the nature of the world and
that permits you to enjoy a detachment that is helpful
to maintaining a healthy body, mind and spirit. This
is hard to describe if you haven't already experienced
it and those who have tried in the past have failed to
convey what happens.

I won't attempt to do it either. It is enough to say that all that is in the world from the table in front of you to the rivers and trees and planets to your greatest love in life is gone, but not in a way that is bad or painful or grief-filled. It is joyous because that elimination is a union, a merging rather than a loss. You learn that all that exists is play, the whole dualistic world is filled with toys for the Divine to play with, which imbues the whole with a sacredness that you rarely feel for the ordinary. It enhances your view of the world as it becomes clear that there is no separation and yet the experience of separation is also a joy because it permits you to experience yourself in another.

It should be remembered that the tantric scriptures that originate in 6th century India have been interpreted in many different ways to try and decode the nature of the universe as it is described there. As a result you have several different tantric sects, some emphasising the female energy in duality and some emphasising male energy. There are some that believe you must move Kundalini (see page 62) energy down from the fontanelle into the Muladhara chakra centre and others, such as my own practice, that works at moving kundalini energy up the spine from the lowest

chakra to the highest. Neither one is better than the other because they both arrive at the same destination, which is the awakening of powerful serpent energy within the body.

Kali worship

The goddess Kali is heavily linked to tantric practices,
in the same that the goddess Tara is for Buddhists.
This is the aspect of the Divine Feminine that is the
womb-tomb, the creator and the destroyer, and this
play of making and unmaking is what is celebrated
in the rituals ascribed to tantric followers. This idea
of creation and death being within the same divine
personage has given rise to many left-hand path
practices (left-hand as opposed to right-hand is the
more difficult path as society would deem their rituals
more beyond the pale). So, for example, a practitioner
might choose to find a human skull at the cremation
ground and use that for a begging bowl. While this
would be abhorrent to those with a more usual morality,
it is a way of remembering the presence of death for
the practitioner who is following that more demanding
path to enlightenment. Again, those who truly
understand tantra do not judge either way as to whether
the left- or the right-hand is the better path to take
towards the ultimate goal. We all arrive there eventually.

Tantra Yoga

Karla Helbert, in her seminal work *Chakras in Grief and Trauma*, correctly identifies an interesting truth about the body's energy centres (chakras): 'In my personal and professional practices, I consider all chakra work to be tantric practice. Tantra yoga involves recognition, expression, movement and balancing of energy throughout the koshas [energetic layers of the body] using mindfulness, awareness, visualization, practice and ritual.'

Mukunda Stiles, an esteemed guide in these practices, writes in his book *Tantra Yoga Secrets*, 'the tantric *sadhana* [practice] is to know your energy, purify yourself of suppressed energy, and promote healthy, energetic expressions that are beneficial to everyone'

Tantra is a branch of yoga that can be said to focus directly on the nature of the Divine Feminine. While it is true that there are Shiva-worshipping tantric sects that emphasise the role of the male Divine, it is a basic principle in all Indian thought that the feminine is the active energy that gives the masculine power to act. Without the feminine principle, the male is impotent. Again, this is not to be confused with talk of sex. It is to do with the order of the universe. For example, in the practice of the 'Indian Feng Shui' Vastu Shastra, Vaastu (note the spelling) is the male plane on which Vastu (*prana* or energy) rests and moves. Each needs the other, but the active, moving force is the Feminine. This can be rather contrary to sexist modern ideas about passivity and the feminine.

Practices and sacred texts of tantra recognize and worship the Divine Feminine principle as the primary source of all power, creation and evolution throughout the universe and all time. This Goddess power is known as Shakti. Tantra teaches us that the physical world in which we live is entirely composed and comprised of divine Shakti energy and, because of this, as we saw earlier, all is sacred. Helbert again: 'Birth and death, creation and destruction, love and loss, joy and grief: all are sacred. When we can see the holiness in everything that surrounds us, including our own bodies as sacred vessels, even the most mundane activities can be treated as ritual to honour Spirit.'

The nature of matter

Energy is arranged in condensed patterns to make up all the matter that we see, as well as ourselves. What we see as solid is merely the agreement of *prana* (energy) to hold that shape for a time. The Vedas call this creative energy *prakriti*, which means 'nature'. It can also be translated to mean 'energy'. This energy is also known as Shakti. This same *prana* makes up and is utilized by our chakras (see page 74). Shakti is also considered Divine Feminine energy manifest. It can be confusing, but stick with it and it will all become clearer as we explore.

In the Hindu pantheon the many gods and goddesses are various aspects of the underlying Shiva/

Shakti absolute (page 21 shows a picture of Shiva and Shakti). As we saw earlier, it is known that the male gods cannot act without their female counterparts. Helbert explains this concept very well: 'They can only exist and witness. It is the feminine that facilitates creation and action. In the tantric view, the concepts of masculine and feminine are very different from those held by western cultures or even modern Indian ones. The masculine power, the witnessing awareness, the pure consciousness of Shiva is by its very nature passive, while the energetic, creative, swirling, ever-expanding, ever-moving energy of Shakti is active. Each needs the other. Without Shakti, Shiva would be content to sit in His pure state of awareness, all-knowing, all-seeing, never moving, never changing, never creating, never engaging. Without Shiva, the kinetic powerful energy of Shakti would not find stability. The matter that Her creative energy generates holds together through the aspect of His awareness. In Their joining, all matter and manner of creation can form and hold.'

Piercing reality

The Hindu scriptures abound with references to *rsis*, a term that has numerous meanings but can be likened to an enlightened person who is also sometimes a teacher or seer that can guide others on their spiritual path. The *rsi* pierces through the notions that we ordinary folks have about the nature of reality and sees the true nature of the play of the universe.

There is a passage in a book called *Principles of Tantra*, written by the orientalist Sir John Woodroffe that highlights how alien the concept might seem to 'normal' people.

He describes how the *rsis* see the world: '...they merely, by the eye of wisdom, in the bed of meditation, in the house of *Sadhana*, see that beauteous dream of the three worlds, and that truth to which the Jiva [living substance] cannot attain even in its causal body, and which, notwithstanding the break of ecstasy, they cannot forget.

'Their vision has, however, this peculiarity: whatever you and I, acquainted with the scientific truths of the gross world, see and think of appears to us to be elevated and of uplifted face, as if nothing else in the *samsara* [mundane world] was more elevated than they; but, on the other hand, the devotees, looking at the reflection cast upon the waves of blood of the causal sea in the womb of Bhagavati, perceive that that which is elevated in this world is low at the feet of Brahmamayi [the Supreme Mother], and that whatever was downcast in the world has, on approaching the Mother, received Her caress and joyfully lifted its head on seeing the Brahman aspect of Anandamayi. The same things are there in both cases. What was seen on land appears again in water, but reversed through change of the medium through which we view it. For those who only see the Brahmanda [division of infinite time] in the Brahmanda, what can be higher to them than it? But those who have seen the Brahmanda in Brahman have seen the Queen of Queens, Brahmamayi, sitting on a throne made of all the highest things of the Brahmanda from the regions of the pole-star, moon, and Brahma to the cloud-piercing peak of Mount

Sumeru on earth. Seeing that all-pervading play of
Shakti which makes the universe stare with wonder,
Devas and *Rsis* have bowed their heads to earth
and said; "Obeisance, obeisance to the Devi who, as
consciousness, pervades the entire universe.

"Is it necessary to say, O great Devi, that She lives in
the bodies of all living creatures when She is present in
the form of energy, even in such lifeless things as stocks
and stones? There is no place in the world where the
substance of Mahamaya is not."

What this rather esoteric passage means is that the
things and people in the world that are reviled as being
'beneath' one are as capable – nay, more so – of seeing
God as those with status and the trappings of our life
here now. It is an uplifting idea, that all may have an
opportunity to pierce the nature of reality and see the
truth beyond.

Samsara

Samsara is the word for the *maya* or illusion of the world. One meaning of the word is 'wandering' and Buddhists and Hindus believe that the cyclic birth and rebirth only ends when enlightenment is reached and so the 'wandering' can end and one can come home to rest in truth.

The great tragedy for us is not that we continue to be rebirthed, but that we have such attachment to our lives as we live them. This means that we do not understand this idea that all life is merely the 'play of the Divine'. We labour under the impression that everything we do, all the status we gain, the worries we have about how other people treat us, the obsessions and addictions, that all of these are fundamental to our identity and sense of self. We cannot let go of these ideas because then, who would we be? We also can't let go of the notion that life should be about the pursuit of pleasure and the avoidance of pain.

The follower of a revered Sufi saint saw that the saint, as he danced down the road, kissed a beautiful girl. The disciple was delighted as he too would follow where his guru led and so he too kissed the girl. Further down the road, the saint took a hot coal from the smith's fire and, with equal equanimity, popped it into his mouth. It was at this point that the follower realised his error. If you are to follow a saint's path, everything becomes One and so the pleasure of kissing a beautiful person is the same as having a burning coal in your mouth. Pleasure/pain, good/bad cease to be opposites and merge into One. The disciple was not ready and, while he wanted the pleasures of being outside the norms of society, he shrank from the pain of it.

This does not mean that the study of tantra will make you impervious to pain, merely that you will cease to be so attached to outcomes. You will never again ruminate on the perceived lack in your life because you will understand that there is no lack. More importantly, you will understand how meaningless this world or *samsara* is for the Great Goddess who can create, preserve and destroy millions of universes in just a glance. The true nature of matter, material, you and your spirit will set you free to never again mourn the shortcomings of *samsara*, in the same way that a child no longer mourns the toys of her youth when she has outgrown them.

The illusion of the world

Woodroffe addresses how difficult this concept is to grasp for modern people in his *Principles of Tantra*: 'To our ears these words, though true, appear somewhat strange. To disregard the joys and sorrows of the visible world, and to be immersed in the joy of the unseen Brahman, is a remote affair. For the present anyone

who avers it seems to be an unsocial, witless fellow.
This advice to run in search of something unseen, in
disregard of the visible phenomenal *samsara*, is thought
to be as unbearable and inopportune as would be
flippant talk to a person who, disconsolate and with
flooding tears, is holding his dead child to his breast, or
as would be a request to accompany a funeral procession
to a young man adorned and joyful on his way to his
marriage. Owing to the unacceptable nature of the
advice, you and I consider the adviser mad, but the
latter is not to be put off from his purpose by that.

'He who knows that all things on the stage of
samsara are merely the materials for the play is not, on
seeing the performance, charmed with the acting, but is
intoxicated with the blissful love of the actor and actress
whose acting it is. *Rsis*, though calm, are yet maddened
by that love; and so they have told us not to waste this
human birth, which is so difficult of attainment, by
thinking of the little things of the *samsara*, but to think
that thought only which will save us from all further
thinking. And, so speaking to himself, the *Sadhana* has
thus expressed the purpose of his heart: "The time of life
(Kala) is past, death (Kala) approaches; let me repair
to solitude. In deep seclusion let me sing the glory of

Kalakamini." The day upon which you and I shall be
on their side, and shall believe or attain the fitness for
believing their word, on that day all thinking will be at
an end. And we, too, shall understand that the *samsara*
is but a mock representation, and that both the things
we see, as well as the people themselves who see, are
She, the Brahmamayi, full of the bliss of the mass of
consciousness who has entered the *samsara* as Jiva, and is
revelling in this joyous play. But because you and I have
not eyes to see, we say: "What sort of a play is this of
yours, O Mother? It is not a play, but the very father of
imprisonment. The first scene of the play is a gathering
on the stage before the actor and actress. Here the actor
is nowhere to be found, so who can find the actress?
With the first act begins the play; next the scenes of
a drama are required. Here, be it the first act or the
last, from beginning to end, the drama is full of scenes.
The scene in which the son appears is that in which
the father disappears. Instantly the curtain is dropped
before the eye, and then who is the son, and who is
the father? You and I have restless hearts, and so we
become disconsolate with weeping. But the very same
play raises weaves of love in the heart of a calm devotee.

Kamalakanta, the peaceful *Sadhana*, has therefore sung as follows:
You know not, O mind, the highest cause
Syama is not always in the form of a woman.
At times assuming the colour of clouds,
She takes on the form of a man.
With dishevelled hair and sword in hand,
She strikes terror into the hearts of the sons of Danu.'

Yet again, what is being requested of the aspiring tantric practitioner is that they see reality for what it is – that both the joys and the sorrows are aspects of the same Divine energy. It is not an insistence that you never feel sorrow or never express joy, more that you understand that these are plays of light reflected on a surface and not the surface itself.

CHAPTER ONE

Scripture and experience

'*Those who preach bookish religion*
are the greatest atheists of all,
because they don't have the slightest
idea of neither God nor religion.
Their beloved religion is their book.
And their God is in the doctrines.'

THE EDUCATION DECREE
ABHIJIT NASKAR

There is an advantage to the written word in that you can read it and then take the time to ponder its meaning and become learned in the subject that you long to understand. However, with tantra the experiential is the most important thing and the scripture merely describes the journey that you are about to take.

For example, this sutra explains the journey of the Atma, or soul, as it rides in the carriage of the body. 'The driver is left to choose whichever path he likes, and to enjoy or suffer from the comforts and discomforts of the path on which his choice may fall. The person driven has neither comfort nor discomfort. Atma is ever free from attachment.'

Since your Atma (or soul) is not attached to the path your life takes, what is the part of you that is discomforted or concerned with the avoidance of a bad path or the taking of a good one? This is what the Buddhists call the Monkey Mind as it leaps restlessly from idea to idea, making judgements and attaching itself first to this concern and then to the next.

One of the most important parts of tantric practice is learning to calm this aspect of ourselves. We do this through meditation and that meditation can take the form of practices that use all of our senses. From the scents we use for reaching an altered state to the sound of mantras or the touch of nyasa (see chapter six, page 162) or the visual aid of mantras and even the taste of sacred offerings.

Many modern self-help gurus speak about the importance of waking up early to improve your life. They are pretty much tapping into an ancient Vedic idea that waking early (between 4am and 5.15am) is the way to greet the Sun God and ensure that your day goes well. For a serious tantric practice, you should also aim to awaken early. Early morning yoga that includes a sun salutation and some time spent in sitting meditation will benefit your practice greatly.

An interesting aside on time. Many of the popular concepts of tantra in the West speak with fascination about sex sessions that go on for hours and hours. This is actually not the case. It is that you step out of time when experiencing sex (or indeed washing the dishes) with a tantric mindset. Time is just another construct of the Divine and when you come into contact with its true nature, you understand that the wheel of time turns at a different pace for each witness. A child may experience time passing very slowly while an old person might feel it slipping swiftly by. As you understand the changeability of its nature, you can stretch or speed it up at will. This is quite the gift as your perception of something dull, such as queuing for a service, or something fun, such as enjoying an ice cream, seem to be long for the former and short for the latter. Wouldn't it be great to be able to switch the two around?

We can't escape time altogether though. We are, after all, human beings tethered to this time continuum. The aspect of time that concerns us most is death. For we soon learn upon our births that death is something that happens to everyone but is nevertheless unwelcome and painful. Most of us live in societies that are ill at ease with death and the meaning of it. We distract ourselves from the knowledge that we and everyone and everything we know will die by acting as though this truth doesn't exist. So we enact plans with no thought to tomorrow. Our current climate change disasters are a result of this sort of short-term thinking. It is better to make one's peace with one's own death and plant acorns for trees that we will never be able to shelter under rather than leave a legacy of poison for those who come after us.

Buddhist tantric practices focus on the importance of an awareness of death. The Buddha himself only realized the ultimate futility of worldly concerns when

he saw the 'four sights'. These are: a sick person; an old
person; a corpse; and a person who has relinquished the
world. Upon seeing these, Buddha left his family to look
for an escape from *samsara* (the world of suffering, decay
and death). Not only did he succeed in that mission,
but he continues to help the rest of us suffering beings
in attaining the same knowledge. We assume that death
means the end of all things – that we disappear along
with our desires, hopes, memories, passions. This is not
the case and Buddhist tantrics work to appreciate and
understand how to die well. The fear of it is removed
when we visualize what it means to die and what will
happen when we do die. It is not a case of morbidly
obsessing over one's death. It is more understanding
death in the context of one's whole life, which renders
it a very small part rather than a looming terror at the
end of it.

To die well in the Buddhist sense requires training,
but a good start is to become more aware of what death
means and become comfortable with the idea that it
will happen to you and to everyone you know.

The Wheel of Life

One of the central motifs in Buddhism concerning
life and death is *Kalachakra*, the Wheel of Life. The
origin of this image is from a story about the Buddha.
King Bimbisara in India was nearly at the point of
enlightenment, but he was unwilling to give up his
kingdom in order to follow Buddhism. To counter
this king's problem with attachment, Buddha ordered
someone to paint the Wheel of Life to gift to him.
Each aspect of the picture was specifically directed
by the Buddha. When it was finished, he sent it to
the king who, upon looking at it, achieved immediate
enlightenment. The Wheel of Life then was painted in
monasteries for monks and worshippers to look at, in
the hope of achieving a similar result. To this day it is
one of the most prominently painted Buddhist wall
paintings. Scholar Kathryn Coster explains it thus:
'The Wheel of Life incorporates all the major concepts
concerning our existence and those of the other five
realms, including the image of our actions having
specific kinds of consequences (karma). In any of the
six realms of *samsara*, we are captives to death (as seen
by Yama, lord of the dead embracing the realms within

the wheel), and only by not undergoing the process of rebirth can we escape Yama's grasp. The Wheel of Life relates all the events of life and death in a concise, logical manner, helping the viewer put his or her life into perspective as well. There's nothing quite like thinking about how everything you have thought or done may affect you when you die.'

Charnel grounds

The physical act of dying is also a key tenet in Buddhist tantra. Our every fibre rebels against getting too intimate with death. We feel revulsion and fear at the sight of a corpse. However, there is wisdom to be had in seeing death up close and personal. Buddhist Monks would visit charnel grounds, burial sites where bodies are left to decompose in the open air attracting animals and being exposed to the weather. Coster writes about this: 'For instance, in India the Buddha advised that in order to gain a true grasp of death, monks should go to these places to mediate life's impermanence and human being's inevitable death. Unfortunately, sometimes on seeing and meditating at the sights, monks were driven to such despair that they committed suicide, which would automatically send them to be reborn in the lower realms. After that happened, Buddha made the physical act of going to the charnel grounds to meditate optional. Meditating on death is not supposed to stimulate fear but a freedom from the fear of death.'

Nevertheless the charnel grounds remain a place of sacredness for tantrics as it is here that you understand the true nature of our physical reality. As the material of the vessels that hold our consciousness breaks down and turns to mulch, we are forced to confront the impermanence of this life and the tragedy of rebirth, when we'll need to do it all again. As we saw earlier, the only way to stop that cycle is to achieve sadhana and cease to keep reincarnating through a profound understanding of our own natures.

Tantric mandalas often depict charnel grounds in the hope that, like the Wheel of Life (see page 40), this will give the viewer pause for thought. Seeing how completely devoid of status, possessions and worldly attachments a corpse is gives the living a template for letting go of their own attachments.

The charnel ground is also the haunt of dakinis, flesh-eating female spirits bedecked in garlands of skulls and bones. They are depicted holding a cleaver in one hand and drinking blood from a kapala, or skull-cup, in the other. While the dakini does not look a particularly friendly personage, in some tantric sects she is a fount of wisdom and liberation. It is believed that dakinis can impart valuable instructions and lessons on the path of right living to those they meet at those burial sites.

Dakinis are strongly associated with the *Anuttarayoga Tantras*, Buddhist tantric text that shows the nature of these spirits is to transmute negative emotions into the luminous light of enlightenment. Much like dense coal can be burned to release warmth and light, they can bring forth illumination from the darkness of ignorance.

It is worth commenting on how much images of dakinis can look like the goddess Kali and the blue form of the goddess Tara. This is because dakinis embody that self-same energy of the Feminine Divine. The ecstatic drinking of blood is a keystone of the story of Kali, who was summoned by Durga to defeat the blood-created demons that were multiplying on the battlefield. Her blood-lust lapped up and destroyed all the demons, but continued apace until her husband Shiva lay before her and she came to her senses.

Beyond the blood intoxication, the cleaver in their hands is also of significance as this symbolises cutting through one's ignorance and getting to the heart of the matter. There are tantric commentators who say that at the highest level of achievement, once the right purifications have been done and the energy body is ready, it is the job of dakinis to come and couple with the devotee permitting them to draw energy up the central energetic spine, into the heart centre, and beyond. This is the point at which Divine Union can occur. So it is important not to fear these entities, despite their terrifying appearance.

Action, not words

Philip Rawson in his *Tantra: The Indian Cult of Ecstasy* writes 'It would be wrong to call tantra a religion; that term has too many misleading overtones nowadays for far too many people. Tantra is not a 'way of thought', either. Thought, in the sense of ordinary logical and very useful reasoning, tantra sees as one of the chief causes for people gradually becoming disillusioned and miserable in what they believe to be their world. So tantra works with action. Above all, tantra is not something meant to be read about in books, although in fact there are numerous Sanskrit books known as Tantras. The earliest, a Buddhist one, probably goes back to the sixth century CE. The most recent are 19th century. But what these texts consist of are prescriptions for action, including mental action, which are the whole purpose of the texts. If you don't do what your tantra describes, then you will never get the point.'

This, in essence, is at the heart of what tantra is – action rather than scripture to follow. Rawson goes on to give an Indian description of a tantric saint as eating forbidden foods, drinking to excess, having ecstatic sex, playing music and weaving it all together into rituals. Everything such a man seems to be and do gives violent offence to the conventionally-minded. And that, in fact, is part – but only part – of the point. For he himself has had to break any lingering attachment he may have had to even his own conventional attitudes. What he is doing fundamentally is taking all the energies he can discover in his body, emotions and mind, and forging from them a vehicle which will carry him towards enlightenment: enlightenment being that state of knowing the truth about the origin of things and people. He does this knowing that the things which you actually do repeatedly, and which have associated with them a powerful sensuous and emotive charge, impact you far more than anything else. However, it is only if you combine together many different kinds of action that the change is radical.

Changing oneself

You are tethered to time. You move forwards from birth to death and experience it going in one direction and mostly feeling fairly even. You understand what a day feels like, even if some days go faster than others. Rawson writes: 'Tantra has always believed that our failure to grasp time lies at the root of all other human failures.' The aim of the tantric is to be able to step outside the constraints of time.

How does one do that? Clearly using the western rationalist model is not going to work. Tantrics have

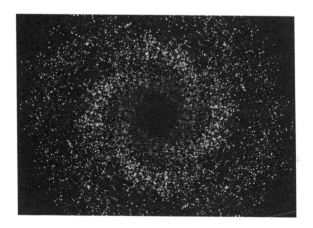

evolved a method of moving up and down the timeline, which is entirely to do with intuitive perception and sense-experience. We spoke earlier about how the ability to stretch time is available to an advanced tantric so that it seems as though an instant lasts an age and an age lasts an instant.

The secret at the heart of this is the breath. As we will see in chapter three (see page 80), it all begins with the breath. The whole of existence is predicated on the in and out breath of the Divine. Everything is made and unmade in that rhythm. Nothing has a beginning and an end – not me, not you, not anything. It is all happening and unhappening. This may be too esoteric an idea to grasp at first thought or it may feel patently untrue as loved ones come to their end or you look back upon your life to date. How can it be true that I am here in this body, subject to ageing, death and decay, and yet I am also ageless, timeless, the mere star stuff of the Gods?

We return to the experiential nature of tantra again. The reason many tantric traditions concentrate on deities, visualising and worshipping them, is because it is a way to recreate the Divine in our image. The male and female aspects of the Divine are gazed upon and the profound becomes personal. It ceases to be remote and incomprehensible. A loving goddess Mother energy can ensure that you reach your goals without losing your mind in contemplation of the immense, impersonal nature of Divinity. You matter. But only in so far as the Divine matters because yet again separation is the illusion, but it is an enjoyable (and very real-feeling) illusion that is created so that you may experience time. The Divine is able to experience time through the dualistic play of the Universe, and so are you.

This experience of living is not your true nature, but tantra permits you to not only continue living as though it were, but also to use the processes of living – breathing, eating, having sex, being in your body, the experience of touch, having emotions, enjoying music – to raise the energy you need to return to contemplation of your true nature at will. The reason the sensuality of tantra is so often at the forefront is that tantrics use all of their senses in the quest for transcendence.

An important example of that is contemplation of the Shri Yantra (see page 55). This sacred mystical tantric design is also sometimes called the Great Goddess Yantra. It is comprised of five downward-facing triangles that represent Shakti and four upward-

facing triangles that represent Shiva. In the centre is the
bindu or centre of the cosmos. It has been said that the
unfolding of all-that-is can be seen in this diagram. To
gaze upon it is to look upon genesis and the creation of
all things.

When seen in its three-dimensional form, it is called
Mahameru, which refers to Mount Meru, the sacred five-
peaked mountain at the centre of all universes. All other
yantras find form from this great or *maha* yantra.

To change one's relationship with time, the senses
are a great ally. Turn to page 55 now and spend a few
moments gazing, in soft-eyed relaxation, at the Shri
Yantra shown there. How does that feel? Are you
immediately trying to 'see' and count all the triangles?
This is another example of the Monkey Mind that needs
to be quietened. Logic, 'proof' or evidence won't get you
there. The wisdom in books, as we have seen, appeals to
the logical part of you whereas what you want to access
is the intuitive, 'feeling' part. There is no substitute for
practice. How would you feel if I told you that a regular
practice of sitting in meditation and staring at the Shri
Yantra would open up the cosmos before you? I have no
doubt that such a sensation would leave you irrevocably
changed as person and as a soul.

In the process of changing yourself and easing the internal chatter of your mind, you will also discover that you have to kill your ego. Our egos care deep about what others think of us and will lead us down the path of falsehood. The story of the origin of Kala Bhairava (pictured opposite) shows that even gods fall victim to ego. It began with a conversation between Brahma (the creator god) and Vishnu (the preserver god) in which Vishnu asked Brahma "who is the supreme creator of the Universe?" and Brahma told Vishnu, with great arrogance, that he should be worshipped as Supreme Creator. Brahma thought to himself "I have five heads and Shiva has five heads. I can do all that Shiva does and therefore I am Shiva." Brahma's ego became inflated and he began to forget the importance of Shiva as well as starting to attempt to take over his work. As a result, Shiva threw a tiny hair from his head which transformed into Kala Bhairava, and this fearsome deity cut off one of Brahma's heads and turned it into his kapala (skull-cup). Images of Kala Bhairava show him holding the kapala in his hand. Brahma's ego was killed and he achieved enlightenment. He was grateful to Shiva for the lesson, returned to his own work, and the order of the Universe was restored.

You don't need to lose your head to kill your ego, merely maintain a regular tantric practice until experiences start to trump mechanical thinking.

The next part of this book deals with practical exercises that you can do to bring tantra into your daily life. Some of these are found within the tantric texts, but others are ones that have been developed for modern living and experiential tantra. It is the case that the tradition is ever-evolving because while the goal remains unchanged, the ways to get to it diversify over time. Take on board those that work for you and feel free to ignore those that don't. This is not the rigour that you will find at a tantric temple, but then again you are not training in the tantric tradition in India so some leeway must be given.

CHAPTER TWO

Modern worship

'There is a super-interesting theory
of evolution: Human beings didn't
evolve from apes. They evolved from
thoughts. Vedas are the original and
purest thoughts that existed before
human beings. Thoughts use human
beings to evolve themselves. Human
beings don't use thoughts.'

ACHARYA SHUNYA

There are several alternative practitioners in the west running workshops around tantra. These usually consist of trying to raise sexual energy through a series of exercises that seem very focused on couples. There is not much space here for the ceremonial or historic ideas around tantra. However, it isn't the case that they have no value at all for many of the practices do aim to raise kundalini energy and that is a start.

Geoffrey Samuel, emeritus professor of religious studies at Cardiff University, defended this neo or pop tantra by writing: 'Tantra as a modern western sexual and spiritual practice, however complex and contested its origins in Asia, was and is more than a fringe phenomenon of the 1960s and 1970s counter-culture. On the contrary, it took up themes of considerable depth and significance within western culture, and synthesized them creatively with borrowings from Buddhist and Hindu sources. Its slow but steady growth since the 1970s suggests that its potential has not yet been exhausted, and I would contend that to dismiss it as an empty and superficial expression of the "spiritual logic of late capitalism" is to miss the possibility of a development of real value.' I am inclined to agree with him as tantra has always been a practice rather than dusty esoterica pinned down in scholarly tomes. If neo tantra leads us to become more deeply aware of what tantra has to offer and to engage with it then it is not a problematic development at all.

Dance as a spiritual awakening

The body is where tantrics – both ancient and modern – focus all their efforts. Most modern tantra workshops begin with some form of movement, whether shaking to 'awaken' the energy within you or dancing free-form to achieve the same purpose. These modern workshops rarely have much to do with traditional tantra teachings because they again focus on the western idea of tantra being about sex and sexuality alone. This means they then tend to aim these workshops at couples and emphasise expressing desire and attraction. Where there is an overlap with more traditional ideas is in the idea of 'awakening kundalini energy'. Kundalini is the coiled serpent in the spine, the miraculous energy that can ignite all of your chakras and give you many physical and spiritual benefits. We often speak of 'unfurling' that serpent and allowing it up the spine and through the chakras to the crown. However, the movement of that energy differs across different tantric traditions – and indeed some sources differ as to its nature and purpose as well. For our purposes, I follow the ideas set out in kundalini yoga. While the term sounds violent, it is

said by some Indian practitioners to be 'exploded' when activated. This is a fairly accurate description of the feeling that arises when kundalini is awakened in one and how instantaneous evolution of the mind and body is when this event occurs.

What is kundalini?

The late yoga teacher and guru, Swami Satyananda Saraswati, revealed that 'the seat of kundalini is a small gland at the base of the spinal cord'. As energy is manipulated to a point of evolution, this gland can be exploded to facilitate immediate enlightenment. This supernatural force has been awakened in rsis, prophets, yogis, siddhas and others across the ages and within different traditions and cultures.

Swami continues: 'In India the entire cultural setup was once organized to facilitate this explosion, but today things are a little different because materialism is a very powerful force, and for the moment, it has even stupefied Indian minds. For the awakening of kundalini, not only are the practices of yoga required. If this awakening is to become a universal event, then the entire social structure has to be reorganized and millions of people all over the world have to be told the purpose of their existence. The whole life from the time of conception to the moment when you leave the body, each and every thing has to be reoriented. This reorientation has to be undertaken with the purpose of expanding the mind and opening new doors of experience. Today we are living in a world where everyone is more or less satisfied. Most humans have all the comforts and everything they need and don't need. There will come a time, however, when people will be prepared to throw off these comforts. Luxury and comfort weaken the will and keep us under constant hypnosis. Alcohol and drugs are not as dangerous as our total slavery to luxury and comfort. We cannot pull ourselves away from them. It is impossible unless we become aware of something more than what our parents and society can give us. Formerly there were only a few seekers, but now millions and millions of people in the world are striving for a higher experience. And this higher experience is known as knowledge.

'When, through yoga and tantra, the awakening of kundalini takes place, a process of metamorphosis occurs in the realm of nature and in the realm of spirit. The elements of the physical body change and the elements of the mental body also. It may be difficult for people of today to understand the whole concept, but soon humanity will comprehend it all. Matter will become unnecessary and insignificant. Behind the matter and behind the mind there is energy and there is an experience of that energy.'

Slow progress

Do not try to push experiences abruptly. You will find here ways to gradually prepare your mind and body for the arousal of kundalini, and advice on basic precautions to be observed in order to avoid unnecessary risks and obstacles. Do not strain your mind, wishing it to comply to some notion of tantric expertise, because, as yogis know, the mind is nothing but an extension of the body. Start systematically with the body, the breath and chakras, as outlined in subsequent chapters. Then build routines as given toward the end of the book, which will enable you to have a daily practice. Then see how you evolve.

Do not turn to mind-altering substances such as drugs or alcohol to enable you to feel as though you are transcending. There are sects who undertake formal rituals in which some substances are taken to aid the process, but without proper supervision and guidance, you will merely be accessing the poisonous aspect of the substance rather than the enhancing aspect of it.

You must also support your body and mind in becoming as healthful as possible before you begin this journey. It is not possible to pour wisdom into a broken vase and expect it not to leak. From your digestive system to your limbs, lungs and bone, every part of you matters. Begin with your diet and go to see an ayurvedic practitioner if you are regularly unwell and don't know why. Invest time, energy and as much money as you can afford into supporting your physical body and bringing it into the best of health.

Swami Saraswati writes: 'The discovery of the great energy began with matter. Did nuclear energy descend from heaven? No, it evolved from crude matter. Where does the experience generate from? From heaven? From the sanctum sanctorum? No, from this body and this nervous system. That is how you should be practical and sensible.' In the following pages, we will attempt to understand in more detail the nature of kundalini energy and how it relates to the chakras, or energy centres, in the body. Then we will move on to how to take ancient ideas of worship and use them in the modern world.

Although kundalini is said to reside in Muladhara chakra, we are all at different stages of evolution, and in some of us kundalini may have already reached Swadhisthana (sacral), Manipura (solar plexus) or Anahata (heart) chakra. If this is so, whatever sadhana or practice you do now might start an awakening in another chakra. However, awakening of kundalini in Muladhara (root) chakra is one thing, and awakening in Sahasrara (crown), the highest centre of the brain, is quite another.

Once the multi-petalled lotus of Sahasrara blossoms, a new consciousness dawns. Even if you do not have a particular sense, this experience is inclusive in its amazing complete transformation. The present, mundane consciousness is reliant on the senses If you are blind, you can never see; if you are deaf, you will never hear. However, when the superconsciousness emerges, experience becomes completely independent of the senses and wisdom infuses everything within you.

Expanding consciousness

Since ancient times, the wise ones have realized that the mind can be expanded and that experiences do not necessarily depend on objective reality. This means that if somebody is playing music, I can hear it, and if somebody has painted a picture, I can see it, but I can also perceive the absence of a picture or music.

'Tantra says that the range of mental experience can be broadened,' writes Swami, 'With the help of the senses, your mind can have an experience based on an object. There can be an experience within the framework of time, space and object, but there can also be an experience beyond the framework of time, space and object. The second form of experience can happen when the present mind expands beyond its given definitions and borders, and when this experience occurs, energy is released from yourself. For hundreds of years, people have been talking about an experience called nirvana, moksha, emancipation, self-realization, salvation or liberation, without understanding it properly. Yogis call this experience samadhi.' Many think that in samadhi or nirvana everything is done and finished. You have complete resolution and can leave ordinary life behind. However, this is not the case. It doesn't finish but one lower level of experience ends and then another higher level of experience begins.

The mystery of this lies in the force called kundalini. This force is pure potential and the fact that it resides in our bodies and has been activated by yogis and tantrics through the ages means that it is quantifiable and provable. We do not need the dogma of scientists to prove that it exists and has specific benefits for the human being because we have enjoyed those benefits over the centuries. You yourself can undertake the journey and hopefully experience the truth of it for yourself. All it takes is time and commitment.

Kali and Durga

When kundalini has just awakened and you are not able to handle it, it is called Kali. When you can handle it and are able to use it for beneficial purposes and you become powerful on account of it, it is called Durga. This is in line with the nature of the two goddess incarnations and their differing appearances.

Kali is naked, black or smoky in colour, and wears a mala of 108 human skulls. Kali's lolling tongue is soaked in blood. The sacrificial sword and the severed head held by the left hand are the symbols of dissolution. Darkness and death are not the absence of light and life, rather, they are their origin. Those who worship Kali see the cosmic power in her accoutrements and know that she represents creative as well as destructive energy.

In Hindu mythology, the awakening of Kali has been described in great detail. Kali emerges in rage with extreme blood-lust and all the gods and demons are scared and apprehensive. She is unpredictable. They send Lord Shiva to pacify her, but Kali roars ferociously, throws him down and stands on his chest with her mouth wide open, hungry for flesh and thirsting for more blood. When prayers are held to pacify Kali, she

becomes calm and quiet. She returns to her Durga aspect.
Durga represents the higher, more refined and benign
symbol of the unconscious.

She is a beautiful goddess seated on a tiger and
has eight hands representing the eightfold elements of
human nature. Durga also wears a mala of human heads,
which symbolize her wisdom and power. These heads are
usually 52 in number, representing the 52 letters of the
Sanskrit alphabet.

Durga removes all evil consequences of life and gives
power and peace, which is released from Muladhara
chakra in her devotees. According to the yogic
philosophy taught by Swami Saraswati, Kali is the first
manifestation of the unconscious. Her appearance shows
that the kundalini is a terrible power and it completely
subdues the individual soul, represented by Her standing
on Lord Shiva.

'When Kali, the unconscious power of man, is
awakened she goes up to meet the further manifestation,
being Durga, the superconscious, bestowing glory and
beauty.' Then both manifestations are combined to aid
the person on their spiritual journey.

Symbolic representation of kundalini

In the tantric texts, kundalini is said to be the primal power or energy. In terms of modern psychology, it can be called the unconscious in man. As we have just discussed, in Hindu mythology, kundalini initially corresponds with the concept of Kali. In the philosophy of Shaivism (a sect within Hinduism), the concept of kundalini is represented by the shivalingam (below), the oval-shaped stone or pillar with a snake coiled around it. However, most commonly, kundalini is illustrated

as a sleeping serpent coiled three and a half times. If you don't like, or are afraid of, snakes, this may be a disturbing image. You can rest assured that there is no actual serpent in the base of your spine! However, it is a very good symbol for your unconscious. We are often very scared of what our hidden motivations and beliefs might be.

In images of Shiva, there are snakes encircling His waist, neck and arms. Kali is also adorned with serpents and Vishnu rests upon a large coiled serpent. It is interesting how universal is the symbol of a snake for hidden knowledge and mystical power. Serpent power is an ancient concept, but you could use any symbol that you are more comfortable with to think about the kundalini. Prana, or energy, has no form and is infinite and so you can visualise it in any way you prefer. This is also the case with colour. The colours we associate with chakras and the energy body are actually quite a recent phenomena and the Hindu scriptures do not stipulate colours when talking about them so, for you, kundalini might be pink, blue, purple or perhaps just white light.

Traditional descriptions of kundalini awakening show it as a coiled snake in the Muladhara chakra and when the snake awakens it uncoils and shoots up through

Sushumna (see page 76), opening the other chakras as it goes. Brahmachari Swami Vyasdev, in his book *Science of the Soul*, describes the awakening of kundalini in the following way: 'Sadhakas have seen the Sushumna in the form of a luminous rod or pillar, a golden yellow snake, or sometimes as a shining black snake about ten inches long with blood red eyes like smouldering charcoal, the front part of the tongue vibrating and shining like lightning, ascending the spinal column.'

The three coils represent the three mantras of Om, which relate to past, present and future as well as the three states of consciousness: waking, sleeping and dreaming. The half coil represents the state of transcendence, where there is neither waking, sleeping nor dreaming. So, the three and a half coils signify the total experience of the universe as well as the experience of transcendence.

Serpent power

Kundalini, or serpent power, does not belong to the physical body, though it is connected to it. Nor is it found in the mental body or the astral body. It lives in the causal body, where the concepts of time, space and object are completely lost. How and where is the concept of kundalini related to the supreme consciousness? The serpent power is considered to arise from the unconscious state in Muladhara. This unconscious awareness of the human then has to pass through different phases and becomes one with the cosmic awareness in the highest realm of existence. The supreme awareness or Shiva is considered to be seated in Sahasrara, the superconscious or transcendental body at the crown of the head. In the Vedas, as well as the Tantras, this supreme seat is called *hiranyagarbha*, the womb of consciousness. It corresponds to the pituitary gland within the brain. Immediately below this centre of supreme consciousness, there is another psychic centre: the third eye or Ajna chakra, which corresponds to the pineal gland. This is the seat of intuitive knowledge. This centre lies on top of the spinal column, at the level of *bhrumadhya*, the eyebrow centre.

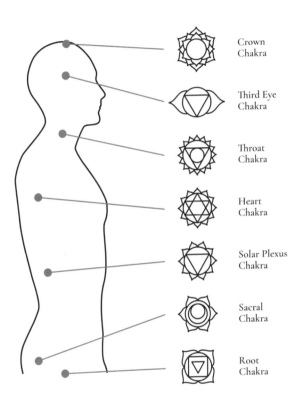

Crown
Chakra

Third Eye
Chakra

Throat
Chakra

Heart
Chakra

Solar Plexus
Chakra

Sacral
Chakra

Root
Chakra

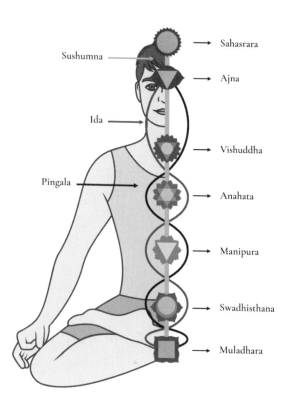

CHAKRAS AND ENERGY CHANNELS

Ajna chakra is important because it is simultaneously connected with the seat of supreme consciousness in Sahasrara and with Muladhara, the seat of the unconscious, at the base of the spine, via Sushumna, the psychic passage within the spinal column. You often see in popular culture that a light shines out of the space between the eyebrows at the third eye location when a film-maker wants to indicate enlightenment. It is because we generally recognise that the third eye chakra has to open to enable that link between the Muladhara and Sahasrara. It is the connecting link between the lowest unconscious seat of power and the highest centre of illumination within the individual. Students often report a tingling sensation at this point in the body when I sometimes lead group chakra meditations.

Swami Saraswati speaks of his yogi practice: 'Kundalini yoga is not abstract. It considers this very physical body as the basis. For a kundalini yogi, the supreme consciousness represents the highest possible manifestation of physical matter in this body. The matter of this physical body is being transformed into subtle forces – such as feeling, thinking, reasoning, remembering, postulating and doubting, in the gradual process of evolution. This psychic, supra-sensory or transcendental power in people is the ultimate point of human evolution.

The chakras

The literal meaning of the word chakra is 'wheel or circle', but in the yogic context a better translation of the Sanskrit word is 'vortex or whirlpool'. The chakras are vortices of psychic energy and they are visualized and experienced as circular movements of energy at particular rates of vibration. In each person there are many chakras, but in the practices of tantra and yoga, only a few principal ones are worked with.

These energy centres are not just physiological but also have a psychic structure that is important to how you experience life. For example, a blocked throat (Vishuddha) chakra will cause you to have difficult communications. You may find that you are unable to voice your concerns and so are often overlooked or unheard. Blockages in the heart chakra (Anahata) will cause emotional problems and stop you connecting with people properly. Each centre governs a different aspect of life. 'These nerve centres are not situated inside the spinal cord itself, says Swami Saraswati, 'but lie like junctions on the interior walls of the spinal column. If you cut the spinal cord transversely at different levels you can see that the grey matter in the cross section resembles the lotus shape and the ascending and descending tracts of nerve fibres correspond to the nadis. These communicating nerve fibres control the different physiological functions of that portion of the body. Many books state that the chakras are reservoirs of power, but this is not true.

'A chakra is like a centrally placed electricity pole from which electrical wires are run to different places, houses and street lights in the vicinity. This arrangement is the same for each of the chakras. The nadis which emerge from each chakra carry prana in both directions. There is a forward and backward pranic motion in the nadis, analogous to the flow of alternating current in electrical wires. The outgoing communication and the incoming reaction enter and leave the chakra in the form of this pranic flow in the corresponding nadis.' We learn more about the nadis in the next chapter.

CHAPTER THREE

Beginning with the breath

'*To breathe properly is
to live properly.*'

ROBIN SHARMA

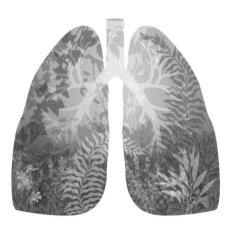

The world is the out-breathing of the Supreme. The goal of tantra is to merge Shiva (masculine energy) and Shakti (feminine energy). Shiva is where all knowledge comes from, while Shakti is the force of manifestation. 'When they separate, duality begins,' explains Sarah Platt-Finger, co-founder of ISHTA Yoga. 'When they merge, there is oneness, also known as samadhi. This is the state beyond time, shape, form, and identity. It is the state of yoga.'

Understanding Shiva and Shakti

Whether we identify as male or female or non-binary, we all have Shiva and Shakti energy within us. Shiva is located at the top of our heads (crown chakra), while Shakti is located in the base of our spines (root chakra). 'When Shakti moves up the body from orgasm, Shakti moves back to Shiva and we access insight, inspiration, and universal intelligence,' Platt-Finger explains.

Tantra teaches us how to direct our sexual energy to connect with Brahma, or universal source energy. If everyone knew how to control this energy and channel it into creativity and higher evolvement, we might not have so much sexual dysfunction in our society. As tantra grows in popularity, it may help heal the masculine and feminine energies that we all encounter within us and in the world around us.

Femininity and masculinity exist wherever there is a description of creation, preservation, and destruction caused by maya through a union of the two persons. The neutral state, or the state beyond that of a male or a female, exists when the aspect above maya is described.

To speak of the neutral does not imply complete absence of the male or the female principle; it implies only an unmanifested or undeveloped state of those principles (Shakti), which can be worshipped only as an undifferentiated mass of consciousness and bliss—primordial, beginningless, worshipped by the Gods and sought by the three worlds.

The tantric breathing practice overleaf, which Platt-Finger taught at Yoga Journal Live, can help move Shakti energy up the body to merge with Shiva to help you achieve oneness.

Tantric Breathing Practice

1 Bhastrika (Bellows Breath)
Breathing in and out vigorously, allow the belly to move out on the inhale and draw back in on the exhale, 27 times. As you breathe out, feel the pelvic floor lifting up, which helps to bring blood flow to that area. Energetically, this technique helps to release the coil of energy known as kundalini (see page 62) that can get stuck at the base of the spine due to unhelpful belief patterns. After 27 rounds of this type of breathing, take a full breath in and hold, retaining the breath. Clamp the abdominal muscles at the lower abdomen and, as you retain the breath, lift and lower the head gently 3-5 times.

2 Release the clamp
With the head down, slowly release the clamp, bringing the palms to face up on the thighs. As you exhale, allow the head to gently come back up. Let your breath return to normal.

3 Ahamkara mudra

Using your right hand, bring your thumb and index finger to touch as if you are pinching something very small, and pierce the point right at the centre of the chest using this mudra (ahamkara mudra). Visualize light expanding from your heart out into each and every cell of your body, and forming into an aura of light around you. Bathe in the light of your own radiance.

Using chakras in breathwork

There are six chakras in the human body that are directly connected with the higher centres of the brain. The first chakra is Muladhara. It is situated in the pelvic floor and corresponds to the coccygeal plexus of nerves. In the masculine body it lies between the urinary and excretory openings, in the form of a small dormant gland termed the perineal body. In the feminine body it is situated inside the posterior surface of the cervix. Muladhara is the first chakra in the spiritual evolution of humans, where one leaves behind animal consciousness and evolves to be a real human being. It is also the last chakra in the completion of animal evolution. It is said that from Muladhara chakra right down to the heels there are other lower chakras which are responsible for the development of the animal and human qualities of instinct and intellect.

From Muladhara chakra upwards lie the chakras which are concerned with illumination and evolution of the higher person. Muladhara chakra has control over the entire range of excretory and sexual functions in people. The second chakra is Swadhisthana, located at the lowest point or termination of the spinal cord. It corresponds to the sacral plexus of nerves and controls the unconscious. The third chakra is Manipura, situated in the spinal column exactly at the level of the navel. It corresponds to the solar plexus and controls the entire processes of digestion, assimilation and temperature regulation in the body. The fourth chakra is Anahata, and it lies in the vertebral column behind the base of the heart, at the level of the depression in the sternum. It corresponds to the cardiac plexus of nerves, and controls the functions of the heart, the lungs, the diaphragm and other organs in this region of the body. The fifth chakra is Vishuddha, which lies at the level of the throat pit in the vertebral column. This chakra corresponds to the cervical plexus of nerves and controls the thyroid complex and also some systems of articulation, the upper palate and the epiglottis. Ajna, the sixth and most important chakra, corresponds to the pineal gland, lying in the midline of the brain directly above the spinal column. This chakra controls the muscles and sexual maturity in people.

Tantra and yoga maintain that Ajna chakra, the
command centre, has complete control over all the
functions of the disciple's life. These six chakras serve
as switches for turning on different parts of the brain.
The awakening which is brought about in the chakras
is conducted to the higher centres in the brain via the
nadis. There are also two higher centres in the brain
which are commonly referred to in kundalini yoga:
Bindu and Sahasrara. Bindu is located at the top back
of the head, where Hindu brahmins keep a tuft of hair.
This is the point where Oneness first divides itself into
many. Bindu feeds the whole optic system.

Sahasrara is the supreme chakra and is the seat of
higher awareness. It is situated at the top of the head
and is physically correlated to the pituitary gland,
which controls each and every gland and system of
the body. As you learn to control and balance your
breathing, each of these chakras will open, permitting
energy to flow through them. The journey of the energy
up the spine takes the road of the nadis. These are
channels for the flow of consciousness and of energy.
They are very important to all tantric work and it is
vital to understand how they function.

Nadis

Nadis are not nerves but rather channels for the flow of consciousness. The literal meaning of nadi is 'flow'. Just as the negative and positive forces of electricity flow through complex circuits, in the same way, prana shakti (vital force) and manas shakti (mental force) flow through every part of our body via these nadis. According to the tantras there are 72,000 or more such channels or networks through which the stimuli flow from one point to another. These 72,000 nadis cover the whole body and through them the inherent rhythms of activity in the different organs of the body are maintained. Within this network of nadis, there are ten main channels, and of these ten, three are most important for they control the flow of prana and consciousness within all the other nadis of the body. These three nadis are called Ida, Pingala and Sushumna. You can see a diagram of these, and how they correlate to the chakras, on page 76. Ida and Pingala are particularly important in balancing the brain and this can be achieved through breathwork.

Ida   Pingala

Channel of awakening

Ida nadi controls all the mental processes while
Pingala nadi controls all the vital processes. Ida is
known as the moon, and Pingala as the sun. A third
nadi, Sushumna, is the channel for the awakening of
spiritual consciousness. Now we see how the different
forces move through these channels: prana shakti (vital
force) – Pingala; manas shakti (mental force)– Ida; and
Atma Shakti (soul force) – Sushumna. You may consider
them as pranic force, mental force and spiritual force.
As Sushumna flows inside the central canal of the
spinal cord, Ida and Pingala simultaneously flow on
the outer surface of the spinal cord, still within the
bony vertebral column. Ida, Pingala and Sushumna
nadis begin in Muladhara (root chakra) in the pelvic
floor. From there, Sushumna flows directly upwards
within the central canal, while Ida passes to the left and
Pingala to the right. At Swadhisthana chakra, or the
sacral plexus, the three nadis come together again and
Ida and Pingala cross over one another. Ida passes up to
the right, Pingala to the left, and Sushumna continues
to flow directly upwards in the central canal. The three
nadis come together again at Manipura chakra, the solar

plexus, and so on. Finally, Ida, Pingala and Sushumna meet in the pineal gland – Ajna chakra.

Ida and Pingala function in the body alternately and not at the same time. Observe your breathing for a minute. You will find that you are not evenly breathing through both your right and your left nostrils. When one is flowing freely, the other is blocked and vice versa. When the left nostril is open, it is the lunar energy or Ida nadi which is flowing. When the right nostril is free, the solar energy or Pingala nadi is flowing. It has been found that when the right nostril is flowing, the left hemisphere of the brain is activated. When the left nostril is flowing, the right hemisphere is activated. This is how the nadis or energy channels control the brain and the events of life and consciousness. Now, if these two energies – prana and chitta, Pingala and Ida, life and consciousness – can be made to function simultaneously, then both hemispheres of the brain can come together and collaborate in the thinking, living, intuitive and regulating processes.

In ordinary life this does not happen because the simultaneous awakening and functioning of life force and consciousness can take place only if the central canal, Sushumna, is connected with kundalini, the source of energy. If Sushumna can be connected in the physical body, it can reactivate the brain cells and create a new physical structure. This physical structure is the aim of the tantrics, for when the body connects with Sushumna and life force and consciousness are operating together, kundalini can rise and you can achieve the state of tantric bliss that you are seeking.

Awakening Sushumna

Sushumna nadi must be awakened in order to serve as a means of communication between higher and lower dimensions of consciousness. When kundalini shakti awakens it passes through Sushumna nadi. The moment awakening takes place in Muladhara chakra, the energy makes headway through Sushumna up to Ajna chakra. Muladhara chakra has been described as a powerful generator. In order to start this generator, you need some sort of pranic energy. This pranic energy is generated through pranayama (yogic breathwork). When you practise pranayama you generate energy and this energy is forced down by a positive pressure which starts the 'generator' in Muladhara. Then this generated energy is pushed upward by a negative pressure and forced up to Ajna chakra. Therefore, awakening of Sushumna is just as important as awakening of kundalini.

Sticking with this analogy, if you have started your generator but have not plugged in the connecting cable, the generator will run but no distribution of electricity will not take place. When only Ida and Pingala are active and not Sushumna, it's like having the positive and negative lines in your electrical cable, but no earth.

When the mind receives the three currents of energy all the lights start working but, if you remove the earth wire, the lights will go down. Energy flows through Ida and Pingala all the time, but that isn't enough. When there is current flowing in Ida, Pingala and Sushumna, then enlightenment can take place. This is how you have to understand the awakening of kundalini, awakening of Sushumna and the union of the three in Ajna chakra.

Shakti travels up Sushumna to become one with Shiva in Sahasrara. When kundalini awakening occurs in Sushumna, awakening occurs in all the stages of life. But if awakening only occurs in Ida or Pingala or in one of the other centres, it is by no means complete. Only when kundalini shakti awakens and travels up the Sushumna passage to Sahasrara is the entire store of higher energy unleashed. You can begin this process with Alternate Nostril Breathing, as shown overleaf.

Alternate Nostril Breathing

- Sit in a comfortable position with your legs crossed.

- Place your left hand on your left knee.

- Lift your right hand up toward your nose.

- Exhale completely and then use your right thumb to close your right nostril.

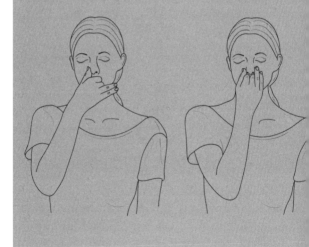

- Inhale through your left nostril and then close the left nostril with your ring finger.

- Open the right nostril and exhale through this side.

- Inhale through the right nostril and then close this nostril.

- Open the left nostril and exhale through the left side.

- This is one cycle.

- Continue for up to 5 minutes.

- Always complete the practice by finishing with an exhale on the left side.

Finding the root

Swami Satyananda Saraswati in his *Introduction to Kundalini and Tantra* reveals the nature of how raising energy up the body is actually getting to the root of yourself. 'In the 15th Chapter of the *Bhagavad Gita* there is a description of the "imperishable tree" which has its roots at the top and its trunk and branches below, growing downwards. He who knows this tree knows the truth. This tree is existing in the structure and function of the human body and nervous system. One must know and climb this paradoxical tree to arrive at the truth.

'It can be understood in this way: the thoughts, the emotions, the distractions and so on, are only the leaves of this tree whose roots are the brain itself and whose trunk is the spinal column. It is said that one has to climb this tree from the top to the bottom if he wishes to cut the roots. This tree seems to be completely topsy-turvy, yet it contains the essence of all occult truth and secret knowledge. It cannot be understood intellectually, but only through progressive spiritual awakening, for spiritual understanding always dawns in a way which is paradoxical and irrational to the faculty of intellect. This same tree is called the "Tree of Life" in

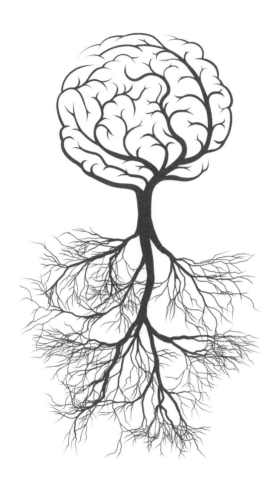

the Kabbalah and the "Tree of Knowledge" in the Bible. Its understanding forms the basis of both Christian and Judaic religious traditions, but unfortunately it has been completely misunderstood by and large, for a very long time. So it is that everybody who is trying to move from Muladhara to Sahasrara is climbing to the root every time, and the root is at the top, the brain, the Sahasrara. Muladhara is not the root centre, or chakra, at all. So if you are moving from Swadhisthana to Sahasrara or from Manipura to Sahasrara, then you are climbing to the root, which is at the top in Sahasrara.'

In kundalini yoga it was discovered that the different parts of the brain are connected to the chakras. Certain areas are connected with Muladhara chakra, others with Swadhisthana, Manipura, Anahata, Vishuddha and Ajna. Just as you use a wall switch to turn on a lamp rather than touching the lamp itself, you don't need to deal directly with the brain but can use the chakras as "switches" to turn on different parts of the brain.

In kundalini yoga the brain's dormant parts are divided into six. The qualities or manifestations of the brain are also sixfold. When you tap into these dormant centres, those qualities can be released. Among the gifts of the brain are psychic abilities, transcendental musical talents and even physical feats that seem almost magical and too good to be true. Fakirs in India have used those abilities not just to power their own spiritual development but also to delight and astound ordinary folk in order to inspire them to begin to understand their true nature and the nature of reality. However, it is not just in India that these miraculous feats have been recorded. We see such magical properties in every corner of the world and, while the names for these people may differ, they are held up as examples to mere mortals of what is achievable when Shakti is awakened.

'A genius is one who has been able to awaken one or more of the dormant areas of the brain,' explains Swami Saraswati. 'People who have flashes of genius are those who have had a momentary awakening in certain circuits of the brain. It is not total awakening. When the total brain wakes up, you become a junior god, an incarnation or embodiment of divinity. There are various types of geniuses – child prodigies, inspired poets, musicians, inventors, prophets, etc. In these people a partial awakening has occurred.

'Although the classical descriptions place heavy emphasis on the awakening of kundalini in Muladhara chakra, there is a widespread misconception that kundalini must be awakened there and made to travel through and awaken all the chakras in turn. In fact, the seat of kundalini is actually Sahasrara. Muladhara is only a manipulating centre or switch, like the other chakras, but it happens to be easier for most people to operate this switch. Each of the chakras is independent; they are not connected with each other. This means, if kundalini shakti awakens in Muladhara, it goes directly to Sahasrara, to a particular centre in the brain. Similarly, from Swadhisthana the shakti passes directly to Sahasrara, from Manipura it goes straight to Sahasrara and so on. Kundalini can be awakened in an individual chakra or it can awaken throughout the whole network of chakras collectively. From each chakra, the awakening shock moves up to the top of Sahasrara. However, the awakening is not sustained and those centres in the brain return to dormancy. This is what is meant by the return of kundalini to Muladhara.' So, while you may have a flash of awakening, it is necessary to maintain your practice to experience it again and in a more lasting way.

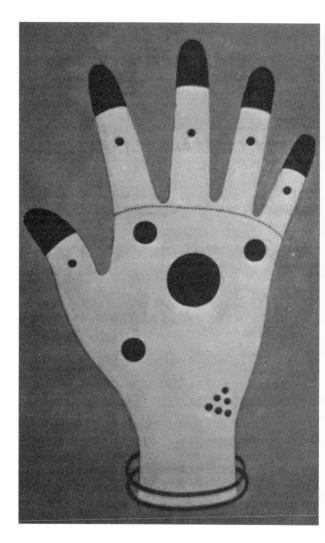

CHAPTER FOUR

Mudras of Power

'*Now understand this, the command and control centre of all these five elements lies in our fingers. So literally, our health lies at our fingertips.*'

MUDRAS FOR BEGINNERS
ADVAIT

Amudra (a Sanskrit word meaning 'seal') is a
symbolic or ritual gesture in Hinduism and
Buddhism. Mudras are sacred gestures and can be used
for a variety of different purposes, from awakening
certain energies in the body to enhancing protection in
a dangerous moment. A fascinating example was when
my daughter once visited a woman at her home and saw
that she had a yantra on a mirror – a surefire way to
create fissures in dimensions. My daughter immediately
used the Buddhist protection mudra of Abhaya –her
right hand placed facing the mirror with all fingers
raised upwards. This afforded her some protection, but
she still fell ill for several weeks afterwards and had
to undertake much spiritual purification in her own
tradition before she was well again.

Some mudras involve the entire body, most are performed with the hands and fingers. Buddha is often depicted using these ritual gestures. There are 108 mudras used in regular tantric rituals and mudras are also used in Indian Classical Dance. There are over 200 mudras in bharatanatyam and over 250 in mohiniattam.

Gyan Mudra

Method: Touch the tip of the thumb to the tip of the index finger, with the other three fingers stretched out. As it is a mudra of knowledge, it enhances wisdom. The tip of thumb has centres to the pituitary and endocrine glands. When we press these centres, the two glands start to work actively.

Benefits: Increases the memory, sharpens brain function. Aids focus and can prevent insomnia. If practised regularly, it will cure many psychological disorders such as anger, anxiety and depression.

Prithvi Mudra

Method: Tip of the ring finger touches the tip of the thumb, with the other three fingers stretched out. This mudra reduces physical weaknesses and makes you more robust in body.

Benefits: It helps if you need to put on weight or muscle. It also improves complexion and makes skin glow. It is great for improving fitness and encouraging greater stamina.

Varuna Mudra

Method: Tip of little finger touches the tip of thumb, with the other three fingers stretched out.
It balances water content in the body and prevents all diseases that can come about due to dehydration.
Benefits: It is a blood purifier since it balances water content in the body. It is also said to prevent the pains of gastroenteritis and stop muscle shrinkage when the body is run down or ill.

Vayu mudra

Method: Keep the index finger on the base of the thumb and press with thumb keeping the other three fingers straight.

It prevents all the diseases that occur due to an imbalance of the air.

Duration: In India, it is believed that the practice of this mudra for 45 minutes reduces the severity of the diseases listed below within 12 to 24 hours. For more lasting results, practice it for two months.

Benefits: It is said to help with rheumatism, arthritis, gout, Parkinson's Disease and paralysis. It is also believed to be useful for cervical spondilytis, paralysis to face, and trapped nerves in the neck. This is in addition to be an aid to resolve trapped wind in the stomach.

Shunya mudra

Method: Keep the middle finger at the mount of Venus and press it with thumb.

It can reinvigorate the body.

Duration: 40 to 60 minutes daily.

Benefits: It has been shown to provide relief from earache within four or five minutes. Any ear-based or hearing problems benefit from this mudra as well as afflictions of the mind, such as rumination.

Surya mudra

Method: Bend the ring finger and press it with thumb. This is connected to the thyroid gland.
Duration: Practice it daily twice for five to 15 minutes.
Benefits: It is believed to reduce cholesterol in the body and helps with weight loss. It can also reduce anxiety and digestion problems.

Prana mudra

Method: Bend ring finger and little finger and touch the tip of thumb with their tips keeping the remaining two fingers stretched.

As it is the mudra of life, it improves vitality and fertility. The weak become strong and blood flows more easily. If practiced regularly, fitness will improve.

Benefits: It improves immunity and the power of the eyes. This mudra reduces eye related diseases It also removes the vitamin deficiency and combats fatigue. While it is in no way a 'cure' for childlessness, regular practice can aid fertility in everyone, due to its overall health-giving properties.

Linga mudra

Method: Interlock the fingers of both the hands and keep the thumb of the left hand vertically straight and encircle it with the thumb and the index finger of the right hand.

This generates heat in the body. Ingest plenty of milk, ghee, water and fruit juices, alongside practising this mudra for the greatest benefit.

Duration: Practice it at any time, but don't overdo it as it does produce a lot of heat in the body. It can cause sweating, even in winter.

Benefits: It stops the production of phlegm and gives power to the lungs. It can be used to combat colds, flu and bronchial infections.

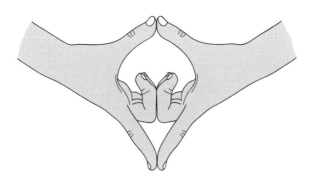

Yoni mudra

Method: The Yoni mudra needs to be performed sat cross-legged on the floor or on a firm chair. Hold your body straight and upright, and close your eyes. Bring the palms of your hands together in the Namaste posture, and point the thumbs up. Now, open your palms apart, while the tips of the fingers of the two hands are still together.

While the tips of the index fingers and the thumbs are still joined, just fold the little fingers, ring fingers, and middle fingers inwards, so that the backs of the fingers from one hand touch those of the other hand. Meanwhile, the two index fingers and the two thumbs form a closed ring (as shown on page 117). Now, press the pointed thumbs against the Manipura chakra at your navel. While you hold this position, breathe slowly and deeply.

The word yoni means 'womb'. It is said that this mudra helps you to achieve the same serenity of mind that an unborn child feels when it is inside the womb. Some practitioners also believe that this mudra helps to improve fertility and also health for the female body. It is also a representative of Shakti, the feminine power.

Duration: Practice this for 20-30 minutes every morning. A word of caution from yogis: if you suffer from a psychological condition such as depression, avoid practising this.

Benefits: Yoni mudra calms the Monkey Mind. If practised regularly, this is a very useful mudra for everyone, regardless of sex, to begin the process of awakening kundalini. This is a very important mudra in kundalini yoga as it seals in pranic energy and is spiritually said to cleanse sins from the body.

It helps in detaching yourself from your senses and untethering yourself from daily concerns. It is a good mudra to practise as part of your morning routine (see page 186) when beginning tantric rituals.

Shiva Linga Mudra

Method: First sit in any easy and comfortable position. Some suggest you sit on a light-coloured yoga mat or carpet to avoid too much heat radiation coming up from the floor. You can leave your eyes open or close them, as per your preference.

Make the shape of a bowl with your left hand. Then place your right hand in a fist on top of your left with your thumb pointing upwards. Ensure the fingers of your left hand are close together. Then hold this mudra at the level of your Manipura (solar plexus) chakra with your elbows slightly forward.

This mudra is named for Lord Shiva and the thumb represents the lingam that is His symbol. It is a very positive mudra that brings light and joy in times of grief and trouble.

Duration: You can do it for as long as four to five minutes a day. Practise it at least three or four times. You can do this mudra pose either in the evening or in the morning time.

Benefits: The benefits of Shiva Linga mudra include heightened energy and reinvigoration. It also produces

heat in the body and so is useful for weight loss. It is not just the heat that it promotes, it is also that all worries are removed and so you get a sense of metaphorical and literal weightlessness.

There is a great sense of positivity and light with this mudra. If you sit in meditation with your eyes closed, you may still find yourself treated to a bit of a light display. Like the Yoni mudra, the Shiva Linga mudra is vitally important in a regular tantric practice.

It can increase libido as well as confidence when out in

public. Because it is not a particularly obvious mudra, you can utilise it discreetly in modern life by doing it in the midst of a business meeting or right before you go to give a speech.

Lord Shiva is known for his ability to destroy and break down those bonds, barriers and behaviours that are no longer serving us and our development. You can call on Him through this mudra to stop any form of self-sabotage or negative action.

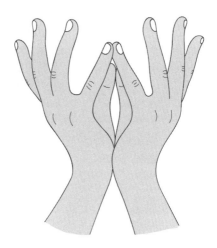

Lotus Mudra

Method: The Lotus mudra is so called because it resembles a blossoming lotus. It is a beautiful mudra to add to your tantric practice. To practice Lotus mudra, bring your hands to anjali mudra (see opposite), or prayer mudra, in front of your Anahata (heart) chakra with the palms of your hands touching. Keeping the heels of your palms touching, your little fingers touching and your thumbs touching as you peel apart the palms of your hands, index, middle and ring fingers away from one another. The three middle fingers of each hand blossom away from one another like a lotus flower in bloom.

Duration: Hold the mudra for five to ten minutes although it is so pleasing that you may find you want to hold it for longer and that's just fine.

Benefits: Just as the lotus flower blooms from the mud so your awareness will blossom as you engage in your regular tantric practice. This mudra helps you to remember your true nature, even as you feel oppressed in the 'mud' and

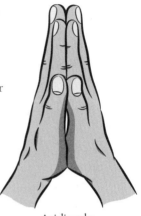

Anjali mudra

muck of mundane daily life. It also inspires love and compassion through your heart chakra and brings tranquillity to a troubled mind.

CHAPTER FIVE

Moving meditation

'*Who is better able to know God than I myself, since He resides in my heart and is the very essence of my being? Such should be the attitude of one who is seeking.*'

THE UPANISHADS
PARAMANANDA

When attempting to begin a tantric practice, it is well to remember that there are as many methods to awaken kundalini as there are people practising tantra. The methods that we are most familiar with include pranayama (breathwork), Raja Yoga and ritual work undertaken either at dedicated temples or modern interpretations of them in western workshops. A basic requirement in each of these – and indeed in the hundreds of ways we haven't yet mentioned in this book – is movement. Whether that is physical movement encouraging energetic movement, or vice versa, you won't be able to get anywhere without shifting things in your body.

You can do this with breathing techniques, meditation, mantras, gazing upon yantras and sacred touch. Yogis tend to divide meditation into either relaxing or active types of practice. Meditating in corpse pose is an example of a relaxing practice. Undertaking to concentrate and remain steady in tree pose is an example of an active meditation. A good practice will always combine the two types so that relaxation is promoted in the body and allows kundalini to naturally unfold, almost as an 'aha!' revelation rather than a forced insistence.

Most research into how meditation impacts the brain has focused on brainwaves, which are divided into four main groups, generally given as follows:

1. **beta:** concentration, logic-orientated thought, worry and tension;

2. **alpha:** relaxation, drowsiness;

3. **theta:** dreaming, creativity;

4. **delta:** deep sleep.

Studies show that most meditation techniques develop relaxation in meditation, with alpha waves being predominant and with occasional bouts of theta waves (which are not the same as those seen in sleep) occurring in more advanced meditators.

The result of accessing these brain waves in meditation has resulted in quite phenomenal changes in health and well-being. For example, the lowering of blood pressure and the elimination of anxiety disorders has meant that many of the world's allopathic medical facilities are now suggesting patients take up meditation as both a preventative and curative method for illnesses impacted by stress.

The real magic though comes from a long and dedicated commitment to meditation. In 1955 researchers Das and Gastant were studying kriya yoga and discovered an amazing thing. On occasion a meditator moves through the usual alpha and theta stages but then develops beta waves. Despite looking perfectly relaxed, the subject's brain was showing alert activity. Even more tellingly, it was not the beta waves you and I might have, which can be chaotic and random. It was big, rhythmic and synchronized. The waves appeared throughout the whole brain showing a level of balance that was highly unusual. The researchers revealed that 'the most striking topographical alteration was the synchronization of anterior and posterior channels' – that the brain's spheres were balanced and pulsating together while the subject was in a deeply meditative state of mind. This would not be of surprise to the tantric but the scientists were baffled.

Banquet, another researcher in the field, confirmed Das and Gastant's findings and came to this conclusion: 'We must deduce, therefore, that the EEG changes of meditation are independent of the interaction between the subject and the outer world but produced by the specific mental activity of the practice. The initiation of the loop between cortex, thalamo-cortical coordinating system and subcortical generators... could account for the different alterations.' The kundalini experience creates the loop that he speaks of here.

Further research found that tantric meditation is not about relaxing the body's nervous system, but in fact arousing it. So ideas that were laid down in 6th century texts are being confirmed by the toys of modern science. The ancients did not need to hook anyone up to a brain scanning device to know that those changes were taking place. A simple confirmation from the disciple that they had journeyed down the same path as their guru was as much 'proof' as anyone needed.

This is not to say that it isn't satisfying to have scientific proof of what happens when kundalini is awakened. The coherence and synchronization of brain waves, in each cerebral hemisphere from front to back and between them is a major aim of tantric meditation and is what happens when we achieve transcendence. This yogic state of ecstasy is brought about by intense concentration but naturally and without strain. The meditator experiences a rush of energy, temperature fluctuations in the body, laughter, a variety of emotions; memory flashes, especially from early childhood; yearning to be one with the Divine; a great sense of connection and understanding of the experience and its meaning. These results were seen in laboratory conditions for meditators who meditated for more than three hours a day. You can imagine how much more profound the feelings must be in a ritual or spiritual setting such as a tantric temple.

An aside about where you meditate – try and do your meditations in one place, so perhaps a dedicated room or area in your home, so that your brain more quickly associates it with the process of meditations that is about to begin. This will speed up your ability to begin to experience the whole brain balance, as described by the researchers.

Kundalini studies

It is difficult, and perhaps impossible, to record the full kundalini experience in the laboratory. Swami Saraswati believes that this is because such advanced meditators do not usually talk about their experiences or the laboratory setting and environment is not correct or our machinery might interfere with or explode under the force of the actual experience.

However, in the studies of meditation in which activation of the nervous system was found, there was generalized coherence and integration of the brain and/or blissful, ecstatic experiences. 'The experiences of awakening of shakti recorded within the laboratory setting and their physiological correlates agree with the yogic theory that awakening takes place in Muladhara chakra and travels up to Ajna chakra, affecting the deep, primitive, animalistic and energizing circuits within the R-complex and limbic system of the brain, near the medulla oblongata. Energy flows from here to the thalamus to stimulate all the areas of the cerebral cortex simultaneously and thereby creates a loop circuit which gradually awakens latent and unused activity within other areas of the

cont'd page 138

Preparatory Meditation

- Sit with your legs crossed on the floor or in any other comfortable posture. Use a chair if floor-sitting is uncomfortable for you.

- Close your eyes and relax your whole body for some time.

- Bring your awareness into your throat and neck. Become aware of the breath in your throat. Concentrate on the sensation of the breath in the throat for some time.

- Now add the awareness of the ingoing breath from the throat downwards. Don't be concerned with the outgoing breath. Your attention should be only with the ingoing breath in the throat. Become aware of the inflowing breath in the throat passing through the network of the diaphragm. Be aware of the diaphragm – the rising and falling of the muscular floor separating the chest and lungs above from the abdominal organs below.

- With each in-breath, it drops into the abdomen a little more, increasing the pressure there and causing the navel to expand. Simultaneously, the lungs are expanding fully in the chest. Be aware with the out-breath that the abdomen contracts, the diaphragm rises and the lungs empty completely.

- Concentrate your awareness in the diaphragm for some time.

- Now, also become aware of the space within which the diaphragm is operating. With the in-going breath, you feel this space is filling up. Just be aware of the process of filling up the space. This process of filling up is the basis for the awareness of this vast space. The process of feeling the breath is only the basis for experiencing the heart space.

- Become aware of the space in the heart; take your awareness directly there. Feel the space within the heart. It is contracting and expanding with the rhythm of your natural breath. The breath is only movement. The filling up happens with the breath.

- Contemplate the nature of the space in your chest. Become aware of the space alone. Feel the contraction and expansion of this vast space – more vast than galaxies. It all rests on the rhythm of the natural breath. The breath is natural and unforced. Do not push it in any way. Do not make it longer or shorter, deeper or more shallow, faster or slower. It has to be a spontaneous and voluntary movement of breath.

- When you become more adept at tapping into this space and understanding this natural breath, you may find that visions come. As you expand and contract each breath, you may find that you experience unusual sensations, deep memories or even visions of water or lotus flowers or deities. Appreciate and thank whatever you receive.

- Maintain your awareness on the in-going breath. Think about its action on the diaphragm. If you are unable to do so, then contemplate that there is a space in your chest that is being filled instead. This is the first stage.

- The second stage is directing your awareness to the space itself and its expansion and contraction on the rhythm of the breath.

- The third stage is the awareness of the blue lotus and the still lake. It will come by itself. Keep yourself ready for that experience.

- Now become aware of the natural inflowing and outflowing breath in the throat. Withdraw your awareness from the heart space and bring it to the natural breath in the throat. Maintain awareness of the in-flowing and out-flowing breath in the throat for some time. Practise this for five to ten minutes.

- Chant *Om* three times. Allow the sound to manifest fully and spontaneously from deep within. For a few minutes, listen carefully for the inner vibration of the sound.

- Release your posture and open your eyes.

brain. The whole brain begins to pulse as a single unit as energy pours into the central controlling area of Ajna chakra.

'We can understand that as we progress in meditation, we set the stage for the eventual awakening of shakti within the nadis, chakras and brain. An explosion occurs as we reach the threshold required for kindling to take place. Once we reach this concentrated, integrated state, neurological circuits take over and spontaneously begin to stimulate themselves so that the energy liberated awakens new centres in the brain, creating a transformed state of awareness and being at a new and higher level of energy. The process of awakening of shakti has begun. From this point on, as long as we continue our practice, the process of unfoldment continues because once kindling has taken place the effects are relatively permanent. We develop more and more purity and strength, so that we can handle the internal experiences as they arise for longer and longer periods of time, until final awakening of kundalini takes place.

'The human brain is truly one of the most awesome and amazing of creations. Housed within the skull, it contains some 12 thousand million cells, and each of these cells has an estimated five hundred thousand possible interconnections; there may be even more that we do not know about. When the mathematics are computed there are more possible interconnections in the brain than there are atoms in the universe. The brain has an almost infinite capacity, and all within the two kilograms or so of amorphous, pinkish grey brain matter with the consistency of jelly or cold oatmeal porridge. How this quivering, pulsating, jelly-like substance remembers, thinks, analyzes, feels, discriminates, intuits, decides, creates and directs all the countless functions of the body, integrating the whole so that we synchronize action, speech and thought, is something that each of us should contemplate daily. Meditation on this miracle of creation, and any attempt to understand how the brain and mind function, can lead to an understanding of the total process of kundalini awakening. Indeed, many of our theories of how kundalini works are based on the brain, and this research can help us to better understand the basis for kundalini awakening, the nadis and chakras. This is because the brain, housing as it does the master control systems for the body within its unlimited circuitry, must contain the physical circuits for the nadis and chakras.'

If you begin a regular practice that incorporates the mudras in chapter four (page 107) and the meditations given throughout this book, your brain will change. It will become the interface between the body, mind and spirit. If you were to do a scan of your brain before your begin this tantric practice and then another at the end of a year of doing it, you would find that your brain has radically shifted from the chaos of a normal 'Monkey Mind' brain to the rhythmic beauty of the brain of an accomplished yogi. One that pulsates with the universe and is beloved by the Divine. Who would not want to entrain their brain with God Themself?

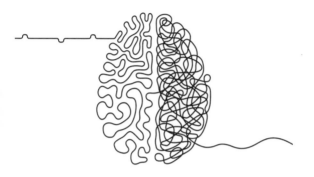

The nadis in the brain

Important research from neuroscience has shown us that the brain fits into the dual nadi model of man's personality as handed down to us by yoga. In a radical and last ditch attempt to cure severe, unremitting epilepsy, Roger Sperry and his associates divided the brains of their patients down the midline structure linking the two brain hemispheres, the corpus callosum. To their surprise, not only did the epileptics cease seizures, but they came up with startling new findings which are radically altering our neurophysiological understanding of how the brain works and are revolutionizing our whole concept of human beings. We have always known that the right side of the brain controls the left side of the body, and vice versa. Sperry's findings, though still in the initial stages and requiring more research, show us that each side of the brain handles a completely opposite but complementary mode of consciousness. This finding is extremely important as it verifies the yogic viewpoint. Yogis and scientists, using different terminology and different approaches, have come up with the same conclusions, that humans are divided into two main modes of functioning.

The circuits of the brain are based on Ida and Pingala, consciousness or knowledge, and action or physical energy. We see Ida and Pingala at all three major levels of the nervous system:

1. **Sensory-motor nervous system (SMS):** all electrical activity in the body moves in one of two directions, into the brain, Ida, and out of the brain, Pingala. Yogis called the sensory nerves which are governed by Ida, *gyanendriyas*, and motor nerves, governed by Pingala, *karmendriyas*. These nerves are concerned with our perception of and activity in the world. They govern parts of movement in the body.

2. Autonomic nervous system (ANS): the autonomic nervous system is divided into the outward directed, stress handling, energy utilizing, Pingala dominant, sympathetic nervous system, or the inwardly directed, rest handling, energy conserving, Ida dominant, parasympathetic nervous system. These two systems control and regulate all the automatic body processes: heart, blood pressure, respiration, digestion, liver and kidney and so on.

3. Central nervous system (CNS): this consists of the brain and spinal cord and contains the controls for the SMS and ANS. The brain contains much more than this though, for it is a huge, ultimately complex computer, which stores and integrates information and puts our decisions into action in a superbly synchronized and orchestrated performance. Its functioning is definitely much more than its parts.

Within the infinite circuitry of the brain resides more potential than we can realize in one lifetime, however, the techniques of yoga systematically clear and strengthen these circuits with regular practice. This is what yogis have been telling us, that the circuitry for nadis and chakras exist within the CNS, along the spine and in the brain. If we can tap, purify, strengthen and reconnect these circuits via the various yogic techniques, we can totally transform our mind/ body complex. The basis for yogic techniques lies in the fact that there is a nadi/chakra system which can be seen, at the physical level, as well as being the sum total of the input and output of the various sections of the nervous system and the parts of the body which connect to it.

This total body/mind complex functions on the power of the three basic types of energy – Ida, Pingala and Sushumna. We can therefore begin to understand why so many yogic techniques are specifically aimed at balancing the Ida/Pingala flow and increasing our awareness of its fluctuations.

Left versus right

Scientific study of the hemispheres of the brain by researchers has shown us that the left side of the brain is usually concerned with speech, logic, analysis, time and linear function, whereas the right side is silent, dark, intuitive, feeling, spatial, holistic in function, and does not require linear, structured analysis for its knowledge. The right side of the brain is the physical side of Ida nadi, and the left brain, of Pingala. Thomas

Hoover, a researcher comparing Zen with the latest neurological discoveries, sums up the situation when he states, 'The hemisphere that speaks does not know; the hemisphere that knows does not speak.' A number of word opposites have been used to describe and help us understand the new view of brain function. Though the situation is not so simple, and each hemisphere must work in an integrated fashion (as the latest evidence seems to suggest), there is a definite trend to separate the modes of function:

Left Brain (Pingala)	Right Brain (Ida)
analysis	understanding
verbal	spatial
temporal	'here and now'
partial	holistic
explicit	implicit
argument	experience
intellect	intuition
logic	emotion
thinking	feeling
active	passive

And we could also add light versus dark, conscious

versus subconscious, talkative versus silent, solar versus lunar, positive versus negative, mathematics versus poetry, rational versus mystical, law versus art, objective versus subjective, digital versus analog, and many other adjectives to aid our understanding.

The greatest mystery is why as humans we wish to split these two hemispheres and opposing ideas rather than having both. We are often caught saying "oh, I'm a left-brain thinker" as if that means we deal with logic and are better than intuitives, or "I'm a right-brain person" to denote that we have more empathy or psychic ability than those boring left-brain people. The truth is that without both sides, you are not a complete person. Without activating and balancing both sides, kundalini will never explode for you and you will never achieve enlightenment. So don't denigrate one side over another. Do your practice and enjoy an holistic experience of life.

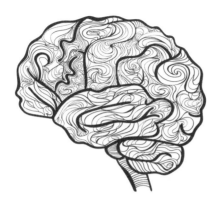

Emotions in the brain

Research on brain functioning points to the fact that the brain has two main modes of emotional activity. The left hemisphere governs happiness and positive feelings and the right brain governs sadness and negative feelings. In an abnormal situation, patients with right brain damage are often cheerful, elated and indifferent to the impact of their injuries. Left brain damage, on the other hand, can lead to a gloomy outlook on life and unjustified anger, guilt and despair.

Most of us fluctuate from one state to another, though not to the extremes found in brain damaged subjects, and this can feel uncomfortable as ultimately our bodies seek balance in all things.

Where the brain's idiosyncrasies become most uncomfortable is in the operation of meditation. You decide to sit down to meditate and from the very first second, you feel emotionally challenged. You may even strain with effort despite feeling good and positive. Your mind tells you how good you are for meditating and having a daily meditation practice. That judgement sets you back four-fold. So then you hunker down and say you will not be egotistical about it and will just let experiences arise as they will. But of course, you're then waiting impatiently for those experiences to arise. The author Leo Babauta wrote the following, excellent practice for ridding yourself of this emotional reliance on making an effort.

Effortless Effort

I've noticed that a lot of us will be pretty wiped out at the end of a long day of work or social activity, to the point where we need time to recuperate from exhaustion.

There's nothing wrong with that, but let's talk about the possibility of doing hard things without exhausting ourselves. We might call it Effortless Effort (similar to 'wu wei' in Daoism) — the idea of acting without a huge amount of tension or extraneous physical effort. When you talk to someone about "trying hard", they usually will put a lot of energy into something and quickly exhaust themselves. "Trying hard" is equated to being very tense, pushing hard with your body and mind, and putting everything you have into it.

If you talk to someone about "relaxing", they will usually think of that as the opposite of "trying hard". They think of lying on the couch, muscles relaxed, not doing anything. "Relaxing" is equated with "laziness" for a lot of people. So "trying hard" and "relaxing" are seen as two opposite things.

What would it be like to try hard while relaxing?

An Experiment

Try this experiment: relax the muscles of your torso, neck, jaw, head … so that you're sitting upright but relaxed. Now read a few sentences of this section, while keeping that upright relaxed posture. Breathe easy, feel peaceful, while reading.

Notice what it's like to give focus to the reading, while not tensing up. While remaining peaceful and relaxed. Now try it while drinking a glass of water, or walking around the room. Upright and relaxed, doing things without spending more effort than is needed.

Practicing and adjusting

We can practice in meditation as well — can you have a relaxed upright posture and keep your focus on the present moment, without straining? Can you rest your attention gently on one spot, not forcing the attention but just resting it?

This is the essence of effort without extra effort. Giving something your focus without spending all your energy. Moving without too much tension. Of course, it takes some tension to move — otherwise you'd collapse on the floor in a puddle. We need to spend some energy to move around a room, or to sit upright. But we don't need to spend more than the minimum required. It's like spending what you need for food, without needing to splurge on every bite.

Sometimes a lot of energy is required. And if so, you try hard with that burst of energy. Just what's needed. And then go back to relaxed upright posture, without needing to spend more. You can practice all day, if you keep 'effortless effort' in mind. You can cook, wash dishes, talk to people, answer email, without needing to be tensed all the time, without needing to exhaust yourself.

Notice if your torso is tensed up, your jaw clenched, your temples tight. Then relax. Notice what it's like to spend just what's needed, and not everything.

Becoming balanced

As we have seen, the brain has two major nodes or systems which must work together and be harmonized. The nadis must be balanced for optimal functioning, for Sushumna to function, and for us to maximize our human potential. Unfortunately, in the west, few of us are really balanced and most tend towards the purely materialistic and technological Pingala side rather than the subtle, intuitive, feeling Ida side.

When imbalance between the nadis is minor, we may not even notice its effect, though it must manifest in our personality, behaviour, relationships and so forth, in ways that are baffling to us, and which can make our lives miserable. Without the right brain we lose our understanding and take things very literally. The right brain, which yogis called Ida or the receptive mind, is vital in the appreciation of relationships, of seeing how the parts fit together as a whole, in understanding.

There is also evidence to show that the right brain is not only important for normal understanding, but also holds the key for intuition and higher experience. Eugene D'Aquili, Professor of Psychiatry at the University of Pennsylvania Medical School, feels that split brain research indicates that the circuits which underlie higher mental states, from flashes of inspiration to altered states of consciousness, lie within the right brain, Ida, and are powered by the emotions. D'Aquili has formulated a neurological description of 'the intuitive perception of God' in which one sees reality as a unified whole, experiencing a feeling of Oneness with the world. He feels it is a product of the parietal-occipital lobe on the right, 'non-dominant' side of the brain which somehow takes over the brain's functioning. Time is experienced as standing still and a sense of absolute and complete unity of self with the cosmos is felt. Both are features of right brain function and this experience is long lasting and totally transforms people's lives so that they find new motivation and a healthier, more fulfilling perspective of their relationship with life. This indicates that unless we begin to take more notice of and develop the right brain, we cannot partake in the experience of higher consciousness. According to yogis, the right and left brain, Ida and Pingala, must be balanced for such experience to take place.

Most of us fluctuate according to our inner biological rhythms, moving from left to right brain, right to left nostril, active to receptive mode, every 90 to 180 minutes. These biological rhythms are well documented though their actual role and significance is not well understood and understanding of how things fit together is still in its infancy.

From the yogic point of view this rhythmic, or in the case of disease, arrhythmic swing, indicates that we are unbalanced and that one mode, one side of our nature is constantly becoming predominant. We rarely experience the more desirable state in which both sides become equal and balanced. According to yoga, when both the sad and happy hemispheres are balanced for a certain length of time, a new state arises which unites logic and intuition, transforms our emotions and enables us to power up a greater range of neurological activity.

We have to understand the necessity for attaining equilibrium and that the resultant state is a better and more pleasant experience. Einstein is an example of a natural yogi who used both sides of his brain. Meditating on what it would be like to ride on a ray of light, he had a sudden and powerful flash of intuition, piercing insight into the mysteries of the universe, indicating right brain function, and was able to harness his left brain to construct a theory of energy and matter conversion which totally revolutionized science and replaced the several hundred year old paradigm of Newton. Einstein stated, 'The real thing is intuition. A thought comes and I may try to express it in words afterwards.' Yogis would say that Einstein had not only experienced the awakening of Shakti in his nadis, but that this initial awakening had also led to activation of a chakra. This powerful experience transformed and enriched not only his life, but many other lives as well.

Perhaps the best known example of non-analytical creative genius is that of Leonardo da Vinci who in 1490 invented a spring-driven car, a helicopter, as well as many other things which came into common usage centuries after his time. His achievements extend into many more fields, and apparently he used his right brain intuition to create an idea, because most of his work is in the form of drawings and visual images rather than in written words.

Of course, there are times when we only require the left brain, for example, while doing a mathematical equation, working on a factory production line, or implementing management policy. However, these things quickly become boring if the right brain is not being used, and such monotonous, repetitious activity can lead to atrophy of our right brain capacities, and even to disease, because such a lifestyle lacks creativity and is meaningless for us. It is minus the right brain's capacity to see meaning in the things we do.

There comes a time when we must bring intuition into our lives, though this does not mean that because we use intuition, we will become another Einstein. Intuition is as commonplace and necessary as eating and breathing. If our lives are to be happy and creative we must bring it into action more. Most situations, in fact, demand it for their proper outcome even though we do not realize it. Even simple situations require intuition, for example, knowing when to shift gears in a car, knowing when a cake in the oven is baked, knowing when it is the right time to say something nice to a friend, or how much strength is required to turn a screw. We have to feel what is required using our right brain. There is no book and no one who can give us this information. There can be no linear-structured analysis of what must be a non-verbal, intuitive knowledge that springs from within, the intuitive flash has no time dimension and defies logic. Within less than a second a total picture can be presented to our mind, the key to unlocking the mysteries of sciences is gained and the seeds for hours and years of inspired work and research may be planted.

For many people intuition is an unknown and unknowable commodity. Years of unhealthy living, lack of direction, purpose and meaning, consistent overstimulation of our sensory nerves, leading to dulling of our senses and an inability to find contentment and satisfaction, plus unresolved, ongoing mental tension and anxiety (unhealthy Ida), added to lack of exercise, sedentary lifestyle and overeating (unhealthy Pingala), all contribute to damaging the intuitive apparatus in the right side of the brain and may even damage the logical, reasoning capacity of the left side. We may find it very difficult to repair and reinstitute function by the normal methods of medicine and psychotherapy.

Thankfully yoga possesses the techniques by which we can rebalance, reintegrate, regenerate and rejuvenate our body/mind complex by bringing about balance in the nadis. We return again to the instruction early on to balance and reinstate the health of our bodies so that we can begin the meditation practice that will awaken kundalini and allow for the healthy action of the nadis and our energy bodies.

Creating balance

Most of us fluctuate from one side of our brain to the other in well documented 90 minute cycles of rest (Ida) and activity (Pingala). A study by Raymond Klein and Roseanne Armitage of the Department of Psychology at Dalhousie University in Nova Scotia found that performance of tasks involving left and right brain activity comes in 90 to 100 minute cycles. For 90 minutes, subjects could do well on right brain tasks and then switch over to doing well in left brain related tasks. This also corresponds with the 90 minute fluctuation in nostril dominance and points to agreement with the yogic theory that there is an intimate relationship between the breath and the brain and their cyclical activity.

If we are unhealthy then our brain cycles may become abnormal in rhythm, duration, quality of function, or in some other way. Our whole life is disturbed and this situation actually occurs much more than any of us, even medical science, has previously realized. Yogis diagnosed dysfunction of brain rhythm by examining the flow of air in the nostrils.

If you begin by doing the Alternate Nostril Breathing as shown on page 98-9, you will discover how balanced you are between your two sides. You may find that you have more difficulty breathing through one nostril over another.

Yogis have repeatedly asserted that there is a strong link between not just the nostrils and the brain but between the eyes and ears and all body organs. Of course, today we know from our anatomy and physiology that this is so, however, yogis were saying the same thing thousands of years ago. In meditative experience they could feel the flows of energy in the nerves moving into and out of the brain and the rest of the body. They were able to perceive even more subtle levels of their being because they invented techniques which developed a great deal of sensitivity and strength. These techniques also allowed them to assert control over the nadis, the brain and all body processes.

There is also research to indicate a definite relationship between eye position and hemispheric dominance. This is why many yogic poses include instruction on where to place the eyes. Gazing straight ahead or cross-eyed toward the nose can create balance in the brain. When we practise these yogic techniques we may feel a very powerful stimulation and pressure within the centre of the head and perhaps even Ajna chakra activation. This feels like a tremendous sense of coming into alignment and a sense of understanding the world and your place in it. This is because energy is shooting up your nadis equally and is being influenced equally by both sides of the brain and body.

Even if your body is imbalanced in some way physically, your energy body can come entirely into alignment. This is why when people have missing limb syndrome and they feel an itch on a leg or arm that isn't there, you can hold a mirror against the limb they do have and scratch that limb to give them relief on the missing leg. Science is unable to explain why anyone should have an itch on a body part that is no longer there, but the connection between your energy body and your brain explains this all very clearly. For all intents and purposes, it is still there as far as your energy body is concerned.

Balanced breathing

If you are unable to hold yogic poses, it may seem as though you will never come into balance enough to enjoy the benefits of tantra. This is simply not true because everything starts with the breath. And that is something all living beings are gifted with. Even plants breathe. As Leo Babauta says, 'simply breathe'.

• If you feel overwhelmed, breathe. It will calm you and release the tensions.

• If you are worried about something coming up, or caught up in something that already happened, breathe. It will bring you back to the present.

• If you are moving too fast, breathe. It will remind you to slow down, and enjoy life more.

Breathe, and enjoy each moment of this life. They're too fleeting and few to waste.

CHAPTER SIX

Nyasa and the art of touch

'*If you want to find the secrets of the universe, think in terms of energy, frequency and vibration.*'

NIKOLA TESLA

Nyasa is a Sanskrit word meaning 'to place' or 'to touch'. In Hindu tantric rituals, it involves a practitioner chanting a specific mantra and mentally 'placing' it within a point on the body – either their own or that of a disciple. Some believe that it is impossible to use a mantra from a book and it should instead be devised by the rsi (sage) to be effective. I have some sympathy for this idea as all we can really do in books is to describe the experience rather than impart it entirely (as we saw in chapter one).

The purpose of nyasa is to place the energy of specific deities in parts of the body, thereby healing the person and increasing their access to divinity. While we do not have access to a sage from the Indian subcontinent for these purposes, you may already have been exposed to nyasa without realising it. Have you ever been to a yoga class at the end of which the teacher asks you to lie in corpse pose on the mat and asks that you bring your attention to each body part and then it relax it in turn? This aspect, called yoga nidra, originally stems from nyasa rituals. As such, you can recreate some nyasa practices for yourself at home.

Nyasa should be performed mentally or traditionally with flowers, or with the thumb and the index finger pinched together as if you were penetrating the body with the most delicate and subtle of touches.

Mantras

Tantric yoga teacher, Tao Semko has written about the use of mantras in both the traditional Hindu tradition and their use in western yoga teaching. 'In Hindu tantric meditations and pujas, the practitioner lays his hands on himself in each of these places, in special sequences. The meditator infuses each location with a special mantra, visualization, or feeling, which is spoken aloud or mentally conjured.

'In the case of nyasa during tantric maithuna (sacred sexuality), the male anoints each part of the female with aromatic oils, ashes, or sandalwood paste, and the touching and mantra infusion both sanctifies each body part, arouses it sensually, and creates empathy, or connection, between the partners.

'In modern western terms, nyasa creates mind-body connections by linking together neural networks, merging physical sensation in the body with thoughts and feelings of sanctity, joy, devotion, protection, and warmth. It is the predecessor (by thousands of years) of the practice of "anchoring" thoughts and behaviours in modern Ericksonian hypnotherapy and in NLP (Neuro-Linguistic Programming).'

In eastern spiritual terms, nyasa is a way to consecrate the body, enhance ritual protection, awaken sensuality in the case of maithuna, and physically meditate on the nature of Divinity.

'Interestingly, the guided relaxations taught at the end of most yoga classes today, and called "yoga nidra" (yogic sleep), were originally complicated mental nyasa, in which the practitioner would relax on her back and mentally "place" the sound of a mantra in each part of her body, accomplishing relaxation, connection, and sanctification all at once.

'In the early 1960s, Swami Satyananda Saraswati of the Bihar School of Yoga decided that the religious overtones of this practice might repel many westerners who might otherwise benefit from yoga. So, by his own admission, he created "yoga nidra" by combining traditional yogic technique with western hypnotic relaxation and the information he read in Herbert Benson's seminal 1960's work *The Relaxation Response*. Before 1960, "yoga nidra" did not exist as you see it in classes today. There was only nyasa, and the dream yoga techniques known as "nidra yoga".'

To experience a simplified, non-religious western nyasa, try Tao's interpretation of nyasa:

1 First, close your eyes visualize a yellow smiley face, just like the ones made popular in the seventies and now seen on email emoticons. A big, happy smiley face right in your palm, and the size of your palm.

2 Look at your imagined yellow smiley face until you start to smile.

3 Now, with your eyes closed, "place" that smiley face in the centre of your chest, by touching your palm to your chest, rubbing your palm in gentle circles, and saying the word "happy" a few times out loud.

4 Then repeat this "placing," this time on your belly, placing the smiley face in your belly by rubbing your belly gently with your palm, visualizing the smiley face laughing out loud, and saying "happy".

5 Feel the results. Notice the changes in your body. Warmth, tingles, circulation, connection, joy?

6 Now repeat the process, touching any part of your body that needs it – sore joints, achy sinuses, whatever. The more you repeat the practice, the more

you can't help smiling – and you'll feel warmth and blood rushing to each area where you "place" the smiley face... Mind-body medicine at its simplest. You can discover more non-religious yogic teaching at his website, taosemko.com.

Nyasa is described in various scriptures such as the *Brihad Yoga Yajnavalkya Smriti* and the *Yogataravali*, as well as many Upanishadic and tantric texts. The *Aruneyi Upanishad* (verse 5) advises all wandering sannyasins to practise nyasa at all times – to chant Om and to place it mentally at different parts of the body. More specific and ritualistic forms of nyasa are described in the *Mahanirvana Tantra*. They include the following:

Matrika nyasa in which the letters of the Sanskrit alphabet (matrikas) are placed on different parts of the physical body of the sadhaka while chanting the corresponding sound.

Hridayadi sadanaa nyasa literally means the placing of the hands on six different parts of the body beginning with the heart. Specific mantras are chanted, for example, when touching the heart chant *namah*.

Kara nyasa in which mantras are placed and chanted on the fingers, thumbs and palms of the hands.

Vyapaka nyasa, all pervasive nyasa. This form is so called because the energy of the mantras is distributed throughout all the parts of the body, together with awareness. Specific mantras are placed and felt on the head, mouth, heart, etc.

A well-known practice is called *angvinyasa* (nyasa of the different limbs of the body). Specific mantras are chanted and associated with different parts of the body. The practice starts as follows:

Small finger: *Om Kannestha Abliyam Namahe*
Ring finger: *Om Anamikastha Abhyam Namahe*
Middle finger: *Om Madhyama Abhyam Namahe*
Index finger: *Om Tarjaneem Abhyam Namahe*
Thumb: *Om Angushtha Abhyam Namahe*

All these methods of nyasa are very powerful. They can be either external where the parts of the body are physically touched, or they can be internal where the mantras and awareness are mentally placed. A vast selection of mantras is utilized, including Tam, Phut, Hrim, Krim, the Gayatri mantra and so forth. The bija (seed) mantras of the chakras can also be utilized – Lam, Vam, Ram, etc. – and rotated throughout the six chakras. The mantra chanting and rotation awareness harmonizes the nervous system, balances pranic flows and renders the mind one-pointed. Each part of the body is systematically charged with the energy of the mantras. The whole body and mind are purified and prepared for meditation.

Yoga nidra has been adapted from the traditional practices of nyasa by Swami Satyananda to meet the needs of modern man. The mantras have been omitted so that yoga nidra can be practised by all people regardless of religion, language and tradition. Though devoid of mantras, yoga nidra has been carefully designed so that it retains its power to transform the personality and receptivity of the practitioner. The emphasis has been transferred from mantra chanting (nyasa) to rotation of awareness (yoga nidra). Mantras such as Om or the guru mantra can, however, be chanted at each centre of the body during yoga nidra if required. Both methods, nyasa and yoga nidra, have their advantages.

If you are not comfortable with chanting mantras but are still interested in the benefits of nyasa, you can also engage in sacred touch.

This is the idea that most westerners turn to when first experiencing tantra in a workshop. One workshop I attended used sacred touch as a way of very gently acknowledging every part of the person being touched. You can do this yourself with a willing partner or to yourself, if you prefer that. You begin by ensuring that you are in a dedicated, warm, comfortable space where you will not be disturbed. You should have ritually bathed first. You then begin at the feet and gently press the person being touched or yourself in a loving and compassionate way. You are seeking just to build connection rather than give a massage or use this as a prelude to sex. You are acknowledging the God in the person before you – whether that is someone else or yourself. You should press with both hands in a gentle way, moving rhythmically up the body, until you reach the face. Here you can switch your touch to gentle stroking and stroke the sides of the face and the top of the head as you would for a most beloved child.

For we are all the children of Divinity and deserve to be honoured in this way. You may find that you burst into tears while doing this sacred touch ritual. Your partner may also weep or fall asleep or become agitated in some way. Note where you are in the body when you get a reaction. This can give you clues as to what is happening in the body. Tender shoulders might indicate a person who has taken on too much. A sore leg could indicate that you are holding on to traumas in your past. Build on your intuitive abilities to sense energy and its movement in the body during this practice. Take on board your learnings and inform your tantric work with what you have discovered.

CHAPTER SEVEN

Daily modern rituals

'*One must observe the proper rites.*'

ANTOINE DE SAINT-EXUPERY

The 55th Patala (verse) of the *Nibandha Tantra* says: '*Gandha* (perfume), *Puspa* (flowers), *Dhupa* (incense), *Dipa* (light), and *Naivedya* (offerings of food). These are the five Upacara. A Sadhaka should always use these five in worshipping his Ishta Devata.' There is a lot to unpack here in terms of unfamiliar words. Upacara means 'sacrament' and a Sadhaka is simply the Sanskrit word for someone who follows a particular spiritual path. Ishta Devata is the deity for whom you would feel the greatest connection and/or the deity you would appeal to for a specific outcome. Interestingly, you don't have to worry about connecting to a personal god in such a case, especially if your beliefs do not permit such a concept. It can be to a teacher or guru of yours who has passed or a saint that you know is the patron for the problem that you are having, or even a mythological idea/thought form that you feel will be helpful to you on your spiritual path. The important thing here is the idea that sacraments can help you connect with helpful spiritual energies in a respectful way. Respect cannot be emphasised enough – to perform any ritual or rite in a non-serious or flippant way is to invite trouble. Honour your beliefs, whatever they may be, so that you do not devolve and lose sight of your destiny.

Gandha (perfume)

Have you ever experienced a complete recall of a memory as a result of a smell? The bath soap your mother used on you as a child suddenly transporting you to being young enough to be bathed? Or perhaps a whiff of the perfume a lover wore immediately putting you in mind of them? This is what the meditative and ritual use of scent aims to do. It is a bridge to experience that is sure and secure. However, you should select the scent you use very carefully because you should ensure you use the same one whenever you are about to sit down in meditation or to do a particular ritual. For example, I know that whenever I am going to engage in sending healing to someone, I rub my hands with jasmine oil that has been diluted in a little almond oil. The scent of jasmine immediately focuses my mind on what I have done thousands and thousands of times before. My brain, body and spirit are ready for the ritual because the scent has alerted them to the fact.

Puspa (flowers)

Flowers are sacred to many different spiritual entities. The sort of flowers you choose are also vital. We know these choices are important because most societies have flowers for celebration and flowers for mourning. We select the type and the colour, according to our own traditions. I once met a shamanic practitioner in the Vodou tradition who never used white roses in any of his rituals because his ancestors had insisted on this. It will depend on what the ritual you are doing is helping with as to which flowers you choose. The scarlet hibiscus was said to be the favoured flower of the tantrics.

Dhupa (incense)

Incense is not quite the same as perfume as the
burning of it brings another element into play and
the smoke arising from incense is another spiritual
sacrament that is due to divinity. Much like the choice
of Gandha, the choice of Dhupa must be appropriate
to the ritual being done.

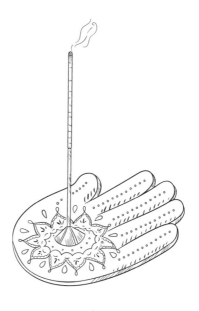

Dipa (light)

Light is an important component of ritual. Even the simplest ritual usually begins with the lighting of a candle. You can use traditional diyas (or Indian oil lamps) for your rituals or a simple tea light. It doesn't matter what medium you introduce light in, but it should include the element of fire. This is one of the ways in which we connect with divinity and the Indian subcontinent has many festivals of light which celebrate the triumph of light (truth) or dark (ignorance). Many Hindu rituals involve moving light around an image – this is called aarti.

Naivedya (offerings of food)

The Vedas say that the gods cannot make food for themselves and depend on humans for nourishment. This is also the case for ancestors. It is therefore important to introduce offerings of food into your ritual practice. This honours your ancestors (and many different religions suggest praying over the favourite foods of departed loved ones and then consuming them brings blessings to them) and, depending on your spiritual practice, is part of the worship of divinity.

Food is a good example of the triple aspect of all energy – creation, preservation and destruction. We make food, we consume it and we expel it. It is a metaphor for the way that the life cycle runs throughout the universe.

While some scriptures stipulate a daily sacrament or offering is necessary, in the modern world we may find we only have time for a weekly ceremony or ritual. This may be a good way to focus the mind on the spiritual, but it is also good to pause before eating on a daily basis and offer thanks to whichever deity you feel connected to, as this is also a way of upholding the idea of sacrificing to God before eating for oneself.

Morning ritual

You will need:

yoga mat

Instructions:

• Begin your day by sitting for some time on your yoga mat and relaxing your body. If you prefer, you can lie down with your legs shoulder width apart, feet falling to the sides, arms to your sides, and your palms turned upwards. In this pose, begin by relaxing your body, bit by bit. Note anything that arises for you.

• Then practice the Alternate Nostril Breathing technique described on page 98-9.

• As you begin your morning ablutions, say exactly what you're doing with each act. For example, you could say, 'I am honouring my teeth and making them strong and healthy' as you begin brushing your teeth; 'I am giving myself the gift of clear

sight' as you put in your
contact lenses; 'I am keeping
my skin clean and healthy'
when you wash your face.

- When you step into the shower, practise the art of
modern nyasa by allowing the water to fall for a
while on your tight shoulders and groggy head.

- Remember to lovingly moisturise your body after
your shower, ensuring you have woken up early
enough to really take your time over this step.

- If you blow dry your hair, really enjoy the
sensation of hot air on your skin.

- Lay out the clothes you want to change into when
you return from work in the evening.

- Begin your day with gratitude for your unique life,
blessing all the people who are around you.

Travelling ritual

You will need:
Clothes laid out the night before

Instructions:

• Wake up early enough to leave the house on time. If possible, leave a bit earlier and avoid the rush.

• Take three deep cleansing breaths, in and out through your nose, as you leave your house. Begin with the intent of having a wonderfully relaxing journey in to work.

• Remember the 'Effortless Effort' practice on pages 148-151 so that you are not mentally straining against the day or the journey.

• Be truly present as you travel. We try to make ourselves absent with music or books or newspapers, but you'd be surprised how much you notice if you keep your eyes and ears open. The universe often has some wonderful surprises in store such as a poster for a play you really want to see or a friend you haven't seen in years. Pay attention to colours around you and really notice details that you might miss normally. For example, do you know the name of the company that makes the panels for your train carriage? I do because I have seen the logo on the floor of the carriage panel. Your mind will begin to consider all the industry and effort that went into creating the system that you're currently using to get to work. Really marvel at the wonders around you and the blessings we enjoy each day of our lives.

Eating ritual

You will need:

Food and drink

Instructions:

• Before you sit down to eat, take three deep cleansing breaths. This will remind your brain that you are now entering ritual mode and must be more mindful and relaxed.

• If you wish, you may incorporate the preparation of the meal into your ritual, by ensuring that you prepare it with great care and presence of mind. Don't chatter away while doing it. Think deeply on the ingredients that it comprises and the sacrifice of the animal if you eat meat or fish. When your food is cooked, take a small amount of it and put it aside on a plate as an offering. (You can eat this later, it is more to dedicate it to the Divine.) You may then consume your own meal, being sure to stay as mindful as possible while you do so. In my tradition, we give thanks for our meal at the end of it rather than before. Give thanks to the Divine Source of all things either at the start or the end of your meal, as per your own tradition.

- If you are eating outside the home, for example your lunch at work, be sure to continue to give your food your full attention. Some tantric practices involve eating fruit with one's eyes closed so that your senses are heightened. Try this every once in a while if you can.

- Go for a mindful walk after you have eaten. This is to aid digestion and to retain a sense of peace. This holds true, even for an evening walk as it will benefit you more than sitting in front of the TV.

- Keep your senses alive to all that is happening around you on this walk and if you can contemplate the joyous feeling of your body moving, all the better.

Evening ritual

Setting up clear boundaries between your public
and private life is what a good evening ritual is all
about. You are getting rid of the stresses of the day
and entering the calm haven that is your home. If
that doesn't sound familiar, try doing this ritual for
a while and see if you can start to get that feeling.

You will need:
Loungewear laid out
Bath oil

Instructions:
- Change your clothes as soon as
  you step through the door.
  Pick the most comfortable
  loungewear possible – a kaftan
  or yoga pants and a T-shirt. The
  point is that you are crossing
  the boundary from public
  working you to private
  domestic you.

- Once you have changed, do three chores, no more. These can be anything at all and some suggestions are running a machine, making dinner, dealing with the mail, spending 15 minutes picking things up and putting them where they belong, dusting, cleaning the toilet or loading/unloading the dishwasher. It doesn't matter what you do, just do no more than three. It is so that you don't have a huge backlog of chores when you should be enjoying your weekend.

- Run yourself a hot bath and put in some really fragrant bath oil.

- Lying in the bath, take three deep cleansing breaths in and out through the nose. Allow the water to ease away your aches and pains. Think about all that went well with your day and how you can replicate the experience the next day. Don't dwell on what didn't go right.

- When you emerge, apply some moisturising cream or oil to your body with care (use the pressing motion described on pages 174-5) and then change back into your loungewear.

- Practice some of the mudras shown in chapter four, starting on page 107.

- Eat your dinner mindfully with your family (see pages 190-1). Avoid drinking alcohol if you can as it is dehydrating and will make you feel groggy the next day. It is also a depressive so if you're already feeling tired and grumpy from your working day, it will exacerbate those feelings.

- After dinner, carefully prepare your lunch for the next day and iron/lay out your clothes for the next day too.

- Keep to a set time for bed and turn the lights down and start preparing for it about half an hour before you're actually in your bed. Try to avoid gadgets and TV in that time as well. This allows your body to know that sleep is coming and to start feeling a bit more tired.

- While you may want to crash in front of your TV (and that is no bad thing), try every once in a while to do something different such as a yoga session at home (use videos if you don't know what to do) or a meditation or go for a walk around the block to get some fresh air and feel the evening breeze on your skin.

Conclusion

'Ask not of plans. Needs the arrow any
plan when it is loosed from the bow?
Such art thou. When the life is lived,
the plan will stand revealed. Till then,
O child of time, know nothing.'

KALI THE MOTHER
SISTER NIVEDITA

There is nothing quite so hard as trying to explain a deeply experiential practice in a book. I am not entirely sure I have succeeded because tantra can't really be taken out of its Indian esoteric context in anything more than a superficial way. Yet this doesn't mean there is no value to western interpretations of tantra or practices that seek to harmonise the energy body and awaken the kundalini.

It just means that you have to do your best and hope that this will result in the experiences you are seeking. I am often asked why, when yogis know so much about the workings of the energy body, we can't just have a very straightforward instruction manual for tantra. This question, on the one hand, is very indicative of the dominance of the Pingala nadi in the person's brain and, on the other hand, can be answered very simply. We do have such a thing! Vedic culture is rich in writings that address all of these concerns, but it is also embedded in religions and societies that are specific to its own history. If you pick and choose the practices and/or divorce them from their origins, you will still see some results because the truth of the energy make-up of humans doesn't change, irrespective of where you are from, but the wider context is lost.

There is a famous scene in the *Bhagavad Gita* in which the warrior Arjun has a conversation on the battlefield with Lord Krishna. He is about to go into battle and is afraid that, in fighting and making many widows, he would be sinning and may be damned to be in hell. This precipitates a fascinating description by Lord Krishna of the nature of the eternal soul and of dharma – a term that can be loosely translated as 'caste duty' but is further a whole societal code of behaviour and morality. Lord Krishna begins by explaining the nature of one's soul and ends by extolling Arjun to battle because to not fight would be dereliction of his duty to God. For a warrior, one's dharma demands that one fights. Arjun accepts the instruction from his guru and goes into battle.

In the same way, as a seeker for spiritual truth, you must seek because that is your dharma. If an imperfect book is unable to get you there, then choose another method. Take up a yogic practice. Study with a tantric guru. Engage in a daily meditation. Most of all, always, always remember to start with the breath. Bless you.

Index

Further Reading

Mudras for Beginners – Advait (Advait, 2015)

Tibetan Tantric Buddhism: Envisioning Death – Coster, Kathryn (2010)

Tantra: The Path of Ecstasy – Georg Feuerstein (Shambala, 1998)

The Chakras in Grief and Trauma: A Tantric Guide to Energetic Wholeness – Karla Helbert (Singing Dragon, 2019)

Tantra for Westerners – Francis King (Aquarian, 1986)

The Supreme Understanding: Reflections on Tantra – Bhagwan Shree Rajneesh (Sheldon, 1975)

Tantra: Enlightenment to Revolution – Imma Ramos (Thames & Hudson, 2020)

The Art of Tantra – Philip Rawson (Thames & Hudson, 1973)

Tantra: The Indian Cult of Ecstasy – Philip Rawson (Thames & Hudson, 1973)

Kundalini Tantra – Swami Satyananda Saraswati (Divine Life, 1994)